Forest Paths
A Manual of Modern Tree Divination

Brian Harrison

Forest Paths
A Manual of Modern Tree Divination

©1999 Brian Harrison

ISBN 186163 0751

Cover design by Paul Mason
Internal & cover illustrations by Simon Rouse

Published by:

Capall Bann Publishing
Freshfields
Chieveley
Berks
RG20 8TF

This book is dedicated to
Mum & Dad
With love and thanks

Acknowledgements

I would like to give thanks to Mark and Mark, Jo, Darren, Penelope and Francis for their encouragement and their helpful and supportive suggestions.

My stepson, Joseph Godber for his wisdom, openness and acceptance.

To Kath, who taught me the importance of trusting my feelings and showed me the power of divination.

Most of all, to Alison, my wife and soulmate. You are my inspiration, my guide and my joy. You introduced me to the tree world and your wisdom and acute perception has influenced every page of this book. You make this journey of discovery a magical adventure and I love it!

Contents

Introduction

The Natural Way of Knowing

In the clambering journey from primitive to civilised culture humanity has sacrificed its connection to the natural world. Our intuitive sense of the spirit of nature has been rejected as superstitious nonsense by the men of science and reason. We have been led in the name of progress to a society programmed like a monstrous machine to strip the earth of its forests and despoil the oceans. While this goes on we in the West insulate ourselves even further from nature in a 'virtual' world constructed from alloy, concrete, plastic and microchips.

As humanity becomes more and more isolated as a species we perpetrate grosser and grosser violations of other creatures. Farm stock is seen as a commodity to be exploited as efficiently as possible. Its suffering cannot be quantified in financial terms and so appears in no balance sheet. Scientists misuse the bodies of animals to perform bizarre and unimaginably cruel experiments. Yet in the depths of our hearts we know that things have gone too far. The so called 'primitive' peoples understood that we share a common destiny with all living things. It is vital that we regain our ability to empathise with animals and plants, rivers and oceans and learn again to hear the living voices of our rich world. The critical carpers who say that this is not logical should ask themselves where their logic has taken us: is it logical to destroy the rain forests that are the lungs of our planet or poison the oceans and soil which are the ultimate source of all life?

And are any of us innocent of this? As I write this on a computer the central heating is on and my stomach is full of food. It is too late to opt out. We are all part of the monster machine. It seems that the only way to escape from this cycle of consumer led exploitation is to renew humanity's connection with the life forms with which we share our world. A good place to start is with trees. To paraphrase Chief Seathl, the sap which courses through the trees carries the most distant memories of humanity. Trees have sheltered and nourished our ancestors. They gave us many gifts including fire and tools. Yet their greatest gift was the inspiration and wisdom that helped humanity to perceive goals beyond survival. Far back in time the patient voice of the tree world spoke to our species of its destiny. In the primordial forests the trees that sheltered our ancestors filled their dreams and visions with pictures of places un-trod, with the desire to explore and the passion to evolve. There are two deep roots that can hold us secure at the edge of this new millennium: our ancestral past and our vast subconscious. From those places the voice of the great trees call to us still.

Trees should be the beloved companions of humanity. We are surrounded by their wood from the cradle to the coffin. The air we breath is alive with the oxygen they make. They are the oldest and largest living beings on the planet and have much to teach us. Yet we have forgotten how to listen. This book has arisen out of my struggle to hear again the voices of nature above the din and clatter of the modern world.

Lyall Watson, in his book 'Gifts of Unknown Things', wrote:

"*I wish there were some way of reconciling formal education and natural knowing. Our inability to do this is a terrible waste of one of our most valuable resources. There is a fund of knowledge, a different kind of information, common to all people everywhere. It is embodied in folklore and superstition, in mythology and old wives' tales. It has been allowed to persist simply because it is seldom taken seriously and has never been seen to be a threat to organised science or religion. It is a threat, because inherent in the natural way of knowing is a sense of rightness that in this time of transition and indecision could serve us very well."*

This book is an attempt to encourage the rediscovery of natural knowing. As Lyall Watson says, the mythology that we have inherited encapsulates a deep wisdom and understanding of the rhythms and secrets of nature. By re-absorbing this mythology we can begin to re-connect to its source: the voices of the natural world.

Rediscovery: A Starting Point

I hope that the reading of this book is not a passive exercise for you. It is hoped that you will find it not only helpful and informative but also challenging and controversial. It is not a work of scholarship and conveys thoughts which have no scholarly justification, just the truth of natural knowing. It is down to you to evaluate what you read and take from this book what you find useful. After reading this book I would hope that you continue to find your own meanings and build your own connections to the trees. In studying the characteristics of each tree you will find that the voice of that tree will become clearer and clearer to you. You will come to learn that trees speak in moods and feelings, rarely in words. You will discover the deep inner peace of sharing space with your tree within the timeless magic of its canopy.

To begin with I suggest that you obtain a notebook in which you can record your own sense of natural knowing. Set aside two or three pages for each tree and record how you feel about that tree. Do any words come to mind when you think of the tree? For example, to most people the Oak is 'strong' and the Birch 'graceful'. Trust your own feelings. Continue to record any insight or new information that you find about that tree.

9

When you discover that tree in your locality write its location on the page relating to that tree. Draw a sketch of the tree and its leaves, do a rubbing of the bark. In this way you will begin to build your own relationship with the trees. It can be surprising to learn how much tree mythology, superstition and stories survives in our culture.

Your notebook can also be used to write down the results of all the divination you do. Re-read your notes from time to time and re-evaluate the messages you were given. In doing this you will expand your understanding of the divinatory meanings of each tree.

At the front of this notebook I suggest that you make some notes that describe where you are starting from. Write the names of the trees that you can identify. How much do you know about them? Do you know any folklore associated with these trees? You will be surprised to see how much tree lore has been passed down to you. Do you ever "touch wood" for luck? Have you ever felt compelled to rest your hand against a tree's trunk or even hug a tree? Do you ever long to sit in the shade of a great tree, carefree? Do you know of any legends about trees? Are you aware of any of the medicinal or herbal cures that can be obtained from trees? What foods do you know of that come from trees? It will be rewarding to return to this record of what you were conscious of knowing before you started to study tree divination. It is surprising how much you can discover about our rich heritage of tree lore in only a few months.

Try to find a specimen of each tree that you can 'adopt' as your personal companion. Take some time to get to know it and observe its changes throughout the seasons. As you acquaint yourself with each tree you will realise how distinct their personalities can be. The feeling in the air around a Silver Birch can be fresh, clear and magical. Willows have a sleepy, somewhat disorienting influence and holly always seems warming. You will be able to use your familiarity with the properties of your adopted trees to enhance your health and well being. If you are feeling low and lifeless then you might feel impelled to spend some time near a high energy tree such as a hazel or rowan. If you are stressed and cannot relax then you would do well to 'crash-out' under the sleepy branches of a big willow.

When you visit your adopted trees give something in return for the energy that they give to you. Tidy any litter from the area around the tree and find a bin for it. Leave some nuts or bread for the birds that live by the tree. You could even give the tree some food by putting a few drops of liquid fertiliser on the soil around it.

You will soon become aware of how the same species of tree can seem very different depending upon its location and surroundings. Trees in heavily landscaped public parks seem less open and more apprehensive than trees that grow in woods. Trees that grow in exposed places have a somewhat stressed feeling about them. Learning to distinguish between these atmospheres will help you to become aware of the fact that every tree, like all living creatures, has an aura. A tree's aura can be sensed as a subtle variation in the air around the tree like a clear mist. Within its aura it is sometimes possible to hear the delicate hum of the tree's song. The tree's aura reflects many aspects of itself: its health, its environment, its age and also its comfort at having you near. Trust your feelings; if you do not feel welcomed by a tree then take the hint and leave it in peace.

In this book I have chosen a specific set of trees from which to build a divinatory system. This selection was designed to do justice to both the ancient traditions of this land and its vital modern influences. You may decide to add other trees that I have not discussed. For example the Sweet and Horse Chestnuts should provide potential associations and resonance from your childhood. Likewise it seems appropriate that a modern British tree oracle should value recently introduced exotic species such as the maple. These add a richness to our landscape and gardens that parallels the richness, variety and vibrancy that has been introduced into our culture by the various waves of immigration that have been occurring in these isles over the past thousand years.

Under each tree I have given the common, botanical and 'Ogham' names. Ogham was the sacred alphabet of the Irish and Gaelic Celts. Each Ogham character was made up of between one and five straight lines cut either vertically or diagonally across a vertical line. This method of lettering was ideal at a time when all lettering was carved on wood or stone.

The individual Ogham letters represented not only a phonetic sound but also a wealth of symbolic associations with the natural world. These associations included myths and legends about birds, plants, trees, men and gods. In this way the Ogham formed an intricate tapestry of information. In some ways it was the Celtic version of a multi-media encyclo-paedia which was stored in the minds of each Druid through an intense training programme lasting twenty years.

The common names are themselves highly resonant, potent and magical symbols. For this reason the tree staves are inscribed with these names alone. The Latin name is useful in that it unambiguously identifies trees which may be known by different names in different places (e.g. the Lime/Linden). The Ogham name is useful in that it hints at the connection that the tree has with places and mythical characters. For example the hazel's Ogham name is Coll, linking it to the Irish King MacColl.

Using Divination to Unlock the Unconscious

A major aim of this book is to encourage the reader to experiment with tree Divination. This would be a good time to say that to me divination does not mean 'predicting the future' but is really about enabling you to see problems from a wider perspective. Drawing on the symbolism and mythology of trees by applying the mythological associations of the trees to everyday life will help you to unlock the rich and diverse wisdom of your subconscious.

The process by which wisdom and creative insight comes from the subconscious was explored by Carl Jung. In '*Man and his Symbols*' he wrote:

"*completely new thought and creative ideas can present themselves from the unconscious - thoughts and ideas that have never been conscious before*". (*Man & His Symbols*, **page 23**)

New insights gained through divination are in fact new only to the conscious mind. The subconscious will already have access to these ideas and awaits only an appropriate symbol with which to inform the conscious mind. The images used in divination provide such symbols. Jung's work on dream symbolism illustrates a parallel method by which the subconscious informs the conscious mind:

"*Dream symbols are the essential message carriers from the instinctive to the rational parts of the mind, and their interpretation enriches the poverty of the consciousness so that it learns to understand again the forgotten language of the instincts*" (ibid. p 37)

Jung was also aware of how symbols often present themselves to us in a mystical way:

"symbols do not occur solely in dreams... It often seems that even inanimate objects co-operate with the unconscious in the arrangement of symbolic patterns" (ibid. p41)

Tarot cards, rune stones, I Ching coins and tree staves are all inanimate objects, yet undoubtedly co-operate with the unconscious in bringing things to the surface.

So the above suggests the following explanation for the value of divination. Divination is the use of symbol systems which allow messages of new thoughts and ideas to be carried from the subconscious into consciousness. The symbol systems used, whether tarot cards, rune stones or tree staves actually co-operate with the subconscious mind to ensure that we are presented with the most appropriate message for that moment in time.

In being drawn to any tree you will be synchronistically connecting to the essence of that tree. In the moments that you share your energy with that tree the depth of symbolism that you instinctively know within yourself can surface. In this there will be a message for you which will tell you exactly what you need to know right now.

The Tree Staves

With this book come cards to represent staves for each of the trees. These will enable you to make an immediate connection with the trees described in this book through the practice of divination. I would encourage you to compile your own set of staves by collecting small fallen twigs from each of the trees. Each twig should be the size and shape of a pencil. Shave back part of the wood and write the tree's name on each stick. It must be emphasised that you should only take fallen twigs. It would be against the whole principle of this book to advocate damaging trees. Another practical reason for only taking fallen twigs is that freshly cut wood will be too wet to

14

mark with the tree's name. An attractive alternative to using wood is to take a leaf from the tree and stick this to a piece of card. Write the name of the tree on the card and some keywords to help you to remember its meaning.

After reading this book I would encourage you to explore your connection with nature further. In your notebook start to compile the mythology of other aspects of the natural world, e.g. birds, wild animals, plants, crystals. Today many people feel a longing to connect with nature but they meet it like strangers, unable to understand its language or hear its message. It is my hope that this book will help you to realise that nature has much to teach us. All we have to do is listen.

How to Use This Book

Walking The Forest Paths

The rational mind solves problems by proceeding in a linear way, coming to conclusions based on established facts. However for this reason the rational mind often becomes stuck. This can happen when there are insufficient facts to go on or there are two attractive alternatives and no logical reason to choose one over the other. The straight track that the mind is on becomes blocked. When this happens it is necessary to adopt curved rather than straight logic and walk around the obstacle blocking our thoughts. Running off from the single straight track of logic there are many paths that snake through the forest of our subconscious mind. Tree divination is a guide to those forest paths. These paths may take the mind far away from the well-worn track of convention and reason and there it may well encounter some strange ideas. Yet among those ideas lie buried treasure.

This is why the apparently irrational act of picking a stave of wood and letting it answer a question can enable you to move on when you feel blocked. By putting reason to one side for a few minutes you are able to tap into the rich resources of your deeper self and gain a new perspective. After that it may be appropriate to step back onto the path of reason. The rational mind can then come into its own and enable you to put your new perspective to practical use. There is an appropriate time for everything (as the Hawthorn counsels).

Finding your 'mission' tree

The following exercise will tell you how you relate to the tree world. Be prepared to be challenged and try to be open to what is revealed. To make any journey it helps to know where you are starting from.

Take your staves and your notebook and find a comfortable and quiet place to sit. Close you eyes and let your mind rest on the gentle rhythm of your breath. When you feel calm imagine the leafy green crown of a great tree. In your mind follow the branches down the trunk into the roots. See the roots burrowing into the rich soil. Follow these roots through the earth until they connect up with the roots of other trees. Imagine this network of roots as a flow of energy. Follow the roots up again to the surface and imagine that this root connects to the trunk of your spine. You are connected to all trees. You are connected to all living things.

Now take your staves. Say silently or aloud:

"Spirits of the trees, tell me now what I need to know about my connection to you and my connection to nature"

Keeping your eyes closed allow your fingers to roam across the tree staves until one seems to 'stick' in your fingers. Take this stave out but do not look at it yet.

Once again connect to your breathing. When you feel ready take a deep breath and gently open your eyes.

The tree that you have selected will tell you how you relate to nature. Read the section on that tree and note anything that seems to resonate with you. Pay particular attention to anything that you feel uncomfortable with, for this is a clue to things that you may be avoiding the need to acknowledge.

The art of using any system of divination such as this lies in understanding how the words given in the book apply to the question concerned. If you are having difficulty applying the answer that you obtained to the question then try to stop working so hard with your logical mind and examine your feelings instead. Did anything that you read conjure up a feeling that seems true to you? Always go with what you feel. What you feel is the truth. The words in the book are only ever a stepping stone to that truth.

If you are still having difficulty deciding how the words answer the question then the following provides examples of how that can be done. Note, however, that this will not give you your answer. Your answer is always personal to you. After reading the example below go back and once again try to find your own truth.

"Spirits of the trees, tell me now what I need to know about my connection to you and my connection to nature:"

The trees say:

Alder   Your expressive power is repressed by social convention and the desire to be safe. The more that you can connect to the wild expansive power of nature, the more open and creative you will be.

Apple   You need to be physically connected to nature, to be out, up to your knees in it. Eating wholesome food and getting out into the fresh air keeps you physically and emotionally healthy.

Ash   You may feel some tension between how you feel that you should lead your life and how you do lead it. You need to resolve this or an underlying sense of guilt will stop you from connecting to nature.

Aspen   You have the ability to sit quietly and hear the messages of nature. Ask yourself whether you give yourself time and permission to do this.

Beech   You have the gist of being able to care for and protect the natural world, possibly by using yours skills at communication.

Birch   You have the gift of being able to enjoy nature with fresh, innocent eyes. If you look more closely you will see the magic.

Blackthorn   You have a calling to nature magic that cannot be ignored. Explore your interests in herbalism and spellcraft.

Elder   You have the ability to take a wide perspective and see nature as a holistic system.

Elm   You should have faith in how much can be achieved by little things. Put your effort into positive actions such as conservation and recycling.

Hawthorn   You are aware of the changing of the seasons and how this affects your energy levels. Use that instinctive awareness to put your energy to its most efficient use.

Hazel   You have the intellectual capacity to develop a keen interest in natural history. You should consider how best to put this to use creatively.

Heather   You see nature as a gift to be treasured and you
                love to be out in the open. You have a very giving
                nature yourself and need to find ways to give
                back to nature.

Holly   You are by nature very active - a 'mover and a
                shaker'. By keeping in touch with nature you will
                find the inner resources to keep this up. Take
                lots of long walks.

Lime   You have a strong sense of right and wrong and
                are committed to ecology and conservation. You
                should use your ability to articulate this because
                you have the ability to influence others to good
                effect.

Oak   You feel the need to be of service to all living
                things. Finding a way to express this need is
                important to you.

Poplar   You appreciate the cycles of nature and are able
                to use this to help yourselves and others under-
                stand and cope with the ups and downs of life.

Rose   Nature holds many secrets. You have the ability
                and inner desire to discover these.

Rowan   You have the gift of being able to connect to the
                spirits of nature. Sit silently by a tree in the open
                countryside, relax and see what they have to tell
                you.

Scots Pine Being close to nature gives you fresh energy and
                illumination.

Silver Fir You have 'green fingers' and a talent for planting
                and growing.

Spruce	You have faith in the natural orderliness and permanence of the natural world but you must avoid being complacent about humanity's capacity to destroy it.
Sycamore	You are intuitively aware of how nature adapts and evolves. This gives you the ability to accept and adapt to the changes that happen around you.
Willow	The spirits of nature will come to you in your dreams. Start to keep a dream diary and look for the messages of nature in the patterns of your dreams.
Yew	You have no illusions about the raw power of nature. However you must not let a fear of it rob you of the joys of life.

If you wish you can repeat the above exercise many times. Each time you do it you will learn more about an aspect of your relationship to nature.

Some Methods of Divination

To gain insight or a new perspective

The above exercise illustrates one way that you can use the tree staves to answer a question. The above method of drawing one stave is useful if you require a new perspective or fresh insight on something. For a more detailed answer three staves could be taken and their meaning combined. For example when writing the introduction to this book I chose the staves Laurel, Lime and Alder. This helped me to realise that the introduction should outline the scope of the book (Laurel is concerned with boundaries); explain the need to foster the feminine intuitive faculties and keep masculine logic and reason in its place (Lime is a very feminine tree); finally to explain the purpose of divination (Alder is the tree of Bran, God of divination).

Before asking a question for yourself, it is always a good idea to write the question down. This will ensure that you are clear about what you are asking: a vague question can only ever produce a vague answer.

To answer a question about the future

If your question concerns the future or decisions that affect it then it is also useful to take three staves but this time as you select the first ask for illumination on the current situation. As you select the second ask for advice about the appropriate action to take in your current situation. As you select the third ask for insight about how this action could shape the future.

A friend was considering taking a job with better prospects which would involve him moving away from home. He had got 'stuck' trying to make his decision. The first stave that he drew was the Aspen. He realised that it was his fear of change that was making it hard for him to see the best course of action. His second stave was Heather. This speaks of the need to rely on other people. From this he concluded that he could successfully cope with the move if he were to trust his friends and new colleagues to be supportive. Finally he drew the Scots Pine. This tree signifies new life and new opportunities. My friend found this highly motivating and took the plunge into a successful new career.

To help in making a decision

It can often be difficult to make a decision when faced with a choice between two or more alternatives which both have an

22

attraction. When this happens select a stave for each alternative. This stave will tell you the hidden pro's and cons inherent in that choice. This alone may help you make your choice, but if necessary draw a further stave to give guidance on what you should consider when deciding what is the best option.

To understand more about a present situation

This can be useful when you want to understand how a situation has come about. Selecting a stave while asking what has led up to the current situation. This can be repeated if you feel that several different things have led up to the present. Draw a final stave to throw light on where you are now.

In some cases it may be useful to select a further stave to give some clue as how best to act. Do not do this, however, until you feel that you have gained a clear idea about your current situation.

As an example of this I asked the staves to help me understand more about why I as a man have difficulties assimilating my feminine qualities and acknowledging my anima. The first stave drawn was the Elder. This indicates what has led up to the situation. This enabled me to realise that the values that I have inherited from my social conditioning have left me with a stagnated view of what qualities should be valued. All of the powerful feminine qualities such as co-operation, intuition, receptivity and magic are completely devalued in this society. The second stave indicated where I am now. I drew the Alder. This made me realise that it is time to question my socialisation and construct a new value system that balances the masculine qualities that help to preserve and protect with the feminine qualities that nurture and create. I drew a final stave to tell me how best to act in this situation. It was the Ash which told me that I must spend time exploring the nature of feminine qualities and having done this re-evaluate what it means to be a man in this day and age.

To conclude this section it must be emphasised that there is no right or wrong way to use the tree staves. However when doing divination I would suggest that you bear the following guidelines in mind:

Ensure that the question is clear. If you are doing a reading for yourself, then write the question down. If for someone else, then give them time to think about what they want to ask. A vague question will tend to produce a vague answer.

Trust your feelings. Always give credence to any image, thought or feeling that you feel within.

Remember that divination cannot predict the future, it can only reveal what is hidden in the present. Be very careful to avoid a fatalistic interpretation of any symbol. Life is full of change and the challenge of life is always to grow and evolve from these changes.

If you are doing a divination for someone else then be very clear about the responsibility that they have given you. Take care in what you say. Do not try to predict the future, especially if it is bad news. Your subconscious only has access to what is hidden in the present and for that reason there is always room for people to shape their own future. Try to express the options available to people, help them to gain a wider perspective on the question in hand and help them by revealing to their conscious mind what their higher self already knows.

Myth, Symbolism and Divination

The Use of Divinatory Systems

The introduction to this book presents a view of divination as something that reveals what is hidden in the present, rather than something that predicts the future. Divination is explained as the use of physical representations of symbolic patterns to allow the subconscious mind to send messages of new thoughts and ideas to the conscious mind. This chapter looks in more detail at this aspect of divination and in particular at the role that myth can play in it.

Myths are highly condensed containers of symbolic meaning and as such are highly evocative. The divination system described in this book is based on the myths associated with trees. The physical representations of the symbols are in our case wooden staves; other systems use tarot cards, I Ching coins, rune stones, dice etc. As Jung discovered, these physical objects actually co-operate with the unconscious mind to present symbolic yet meaningful patterns to the conscious mind. The previous sentence will seem controversial to the logical mind, but can be confirmed by the many people who have used divinatory systems over the centuries.

For these reasons successful tree divination can be done using tokens of the given trees even if those tokens do not contain wood from the actual trees themselves. Any token such as a card which shows a picture or a name of the tree already contain potent symbols of the tree and as such will allow the unconscious mind to send messages to the conscious mind. If you endeavor to make your own tokens from wood of the actual trees themselves then you will be more closely attuned to the energy and personality of each of the trees. However the unconscious mind will not stand and wait for you to do this. It will make use of whatever symbols it has at hand to continue to guide the personality and will readily use a token of each tree such as a card with its name on.

Symbols and subjectivity

Symbols are subjective. This has a number of implications for us. The first thing to note is that symbols can mean different things in different contexts and different things to different people. Hence any attempt to describe the message and meaning of any symbol must be qualified by the context of the question and the person asking it. Anyone using a divinatory system must remain open to this, just as anyone traveling abroad should be sensitive to the fact that a gesture that means one thing at home may mean something quite different elsewhere.

Superficially this would imply that if the person asking the question is interpreting their own divination then they will be more likely to correctly interpret the symbols that come up. However this is not usually the case, as any experienced tarot reader will know. This difficulty in doing your own readings arises for the same reason that it is difficult to interpret your own dreams: the conscious mind has a natural tendency to deliberately block and ignore the messages of the unconscious. However if an independent person can sensitively point out the distinguishing symbolic patterns of a reading, taking care not to impose a pre-conceived meaning but rather enable the person with the question to tease out the significance of these symbols for themselves, then a divinatory system can be a powerful means of broadening the understanding, perspective and knowledge of the person with the question.

The role of the unconscious psyche

A second implication of this view of how divination works is that taking a logical, rational approach to interpreting the meanings of the divination is futile. Just as the physical object used in the reading will collude with the unconscious of the person with the question, the unconscious mind of the reader also colludes with the questioners unconscious. Successful 'fortune tellers' have the ability to speak from their unconscious psyche. This is the true source of 'psychic' ability.

I would like to stress that I do not think that this psychological explanation of psychic ability reduces psychic phenomena to a scientific theory. Indeed it underlines the deep mysteries involved. Two fundamental questions remain unanswered: how can physical objects 'collude' with the unconscious and how can one person's unconscious psyche know things about another person that there is no causal reason for them to know?

For now I shall leave these mysteries unprobed. It seems fitting that the Goddess should remain veiled. The key point here is that the 'reader' must access the resources of their unconscious psyche if they are to help the person asking the question to become 'unstuck'. They must be very wary of letting their conscious side (their 'ego') get in the way by presenting a rationalized explanation of the symbols to the questioner.

Tree myths

The myths associated with each tree are themselves extended symbols representing deep truths about life. They have been passed down and refined over many generations and have even traversed civilizations. Hence these myths provide a potent source of material for the unconscious mind to work with. For this reason I would recommend then when doing divination using the tree staves you tell the questioner not only the divinatory meanings of the trees but also the myths associated with them. In this way even if the conscious mind of the questioner does not relate to what you have said their unconscious psyche will be activated and enriched. It is likely that the significance of these myths will come to the questioner later in their dreams. Advise people to record their dreams after you have done a reading for them and then see if these can be related back to the myths presented by the trees.

Many divinatory systems are built around the telling of symbolic stories or myths. The figures in the tarot cards express highly evocative stories. The Chinese oracular system 'I Ching' is composed of a series of epigrammatic tales. Other systems do not seem to rely so heavily on myth but still rely heavily on symbolism. For example systems of numerology and 'dice' rolling are based on the deeply ingrained symbolism that numbers have attached to them. Likewise when ordinary playing cards are used for 'fortune telling' the reader relies heavily on the symbolism associated with each number, the suits and the picture cards. It seems that the most successful and popular divinatory systems are ones whose truths are bound up with physical representations of myths and symbols.

Archetypes, the collective unconscious and synchronicity

In addition to each person's individual unconscious Jung proposed that there is a 'collective' unconscious shared by people across different cultures and times. He called the symbols of the collective unconscious 'archetypes'. Trees, tarot cards etc. are not in themselves archetypes but are a very special sort of symbol that represent archetypes. For example the archetype 'great mother' recurs throughout all cultures. In the tarot this archetype is represented by the Empress card. In the Tree world it is represented by the Elder.

The relevance of this to divination is as follows. Given that the physical objects used in divination represent archetypal images then they not only allow communication between the conscious and unconscious mind but also they allow communication between the individual and collective unconscious.

In his introduction to the I Ching Jung says that *"Synchronicity takes the coincidence of events in space and time as meaning something more than mere chance, namely, a peculiar interdependence of objective events among themselves as well as with the subjective (psychic) states of the observer or observers"* (Wilhelm page CCLV)

The theory of synchronicity begins to explain the mechanism behind how physical objects can collude with the unconscious to inform the conscious mind. Have you ever had the experience of picking a book at random and finding that it was exactly what you needed to read? Have you ever been thinking of someone when the phone rings and it was that very person. These are examples of synchronous events. For Jung such events are not the result of pure chance or coincidence. They point to the fact that seemingly unconnected events are linked together in a web of mutually significant and symbolic patterns. It was for this reason that Jung became fascinated by astrology. Astrology itself is based on the premise that the seemingly unconnected relationships of the planets at the time of birth presents a symbolic pattern which can be interpreted to reveal meaningful information about a person.

Tree, Myth, Symbol

The above can be drawn together into an analysis of one of the ways in which the tree divination systems work. The tree staves collude with the subconscious mind to enable the most significant tree stave or staves to be selected. These trees are associated with a variety of myths which themselves represent a wealth of symbolism. It is by use of symbolism that the subconscious mind communicates with the conscious mind. In this manner the conscious mind becomes informed or gains a new or creative perspective.

It might be more appropriate to refer to the subconscious mind as the 'super' conscious. The above description of its role in informing the conscious mind credits it with much subtlety. This view is central to the psychology of Carl Jung. Jung revealed much of interest but his idea most relevant to the matter in hand is the discovery that the conscious personality is, like the tip of an iceberg, only a small part of our whole personality. The bulk of our being is made up of our unconscious psyche. This unconscious is in no way inferior to the conscious. It is in fact much more in touch with our real needs than the conscious mind. For this reason Jung preferred to use the word 'unconscious' rather than the term 'subconscious' which Freud used, suggesting something inferior to the conscious mind.

The anima and animus

Jung's psychological theories throw light on various aspects of divinatory systems. For example some of the most popular systems include strong images of men and women. The tarot cards depict a variety of strong male and female figures. Likewise many of the myths associated with trees relate to Gods & Goddesses.

To Jung each of us have within ourselves a buried contrasexual self. Men have an anima, a hidden persona which exhibits their female qualities. Likewise woman have an animus, their hidden male.

When we select a tree (or tarot card) that is strongly associated with the opposite sex to ourselves then this is a sign that our anima/animus is communicating with us. We must approach the matter in hand with in a more balanced manner, applying both our masculine and feminine sides to it.

In our patriarchal society positive strong images of feminine power are suppressed. This undermines the ability of women to connect with their feminine power. It also makes it difficult for men to acknowledge the feminine qualities within themselves, for they have been conditioned to view such qualities as sign of weakness. This is unsurprising given that patriarchy has replaced the true images of feminine power with pale characatures of what it is to be a woman. These caricatures are nowadays blatantly re-inforced by the advertisers, the tabloid media and the film industry.

If we, men and women alike, seek to retrieve the true image of femininity then the ancient myths are a good place to start. Likewise the trees also have much to teach. The graceful birch is the most hardy of trees, the wiry elder the most healing. Together they represent the Bright and the Dark Maiden who together are Diana, the Goddess of the Waxing and the Waning Moon, the untamed huntress who chooses her own lovers and roams the wild places of our souls.

Alder

Latin name: *Alnus glutinosa*
Ogham name: Fearn

The alder inhabits watery places and uses the waters of rivers and streams to disperse its seeds. It often has more than one trunk rising straight and high into the crown of the tree. The alder is the only deciduous tree to have cones. Alders live in symbiosis with bacteria that reside in nodules on the roots and absorb nitrogen from the air. The leakage of this nitrogen from the roots improves the soil around the tree.

Alder is known as the 'King of the Waters'. The wood is oily which makes it very resistant to decay when in water. For this reason it was used to build bridges and the foundations of buildings built in water. Many buildings in Venice are constructed on alder piles. The wood was also used to make milk churns. Its water resistant qualities may have been a reason for this but folk lore has it that the wood protects the milk from going sour if hexed by witches. Witches were also reputed to use alder pipes to whistle up the bitterly cold north wind.

The tree's sap turns red when exposed to air, so when chopped down the tree looks as if it is bleeding. Alder's water-proof wood and its red sap led to the belief that the tree contained a fiery energy. It also makes an excellent charcoal. This fiery quality led to the belief that cutting down an alder would lead to your house being burned down.

Alder was a sacred tree in many cultures. It is the totem tree of the Celtic God Bran. In one legend Bran became a bridge, reflecting the fact that alder is ideal for constructions built in water. Bran was known as 'Bran of the Wondrous Head'. He was the God of the Druid's sacred head cult, which believed that human skulls were a source of prophecy and omens. Bran's head was said to have been buried under the White Mount at the Tower of London where it was guarded by ravens. Ravens and crows are another symbol of oracular power.

The presence of ravens at the Tower of London illustrates the persistence of ancient mythology in the national psyche. Legend has it that Britain will be invaded when the ravens leave the Tower. For this reason Prime Minister Winston Churchill, during the Second World War, ordered that ravens be taken to the grounds of the Tower. The ravens are still there, a popular tourist attraction. Ravens, whose presence at the Tower symbolise the intact sovereignty of Britain, were also the bird of the God Bran. Bran was the Alder God. Alder is the tree of sovereignty and foundations. This demonstrates how myth and history intertwine in our consciousness to create heavily laden symbolism.

The alder, the crow and divination were also symbols and attributes of the Greek God Cronus. Cronus was the son of the earth mother Gaia and Uranus. Cronus took his father's sovereignty, symbolically castrating him. Cronus himself was usurped by his own son, Zeus.

The tree is said to provide spiritual protection, especially in the midst of quarrels and disputes.

It seems appropriate that the first tree of this book, its foundation, is the alder since the alder is the tree of divination and of foundations.

In summary the key qualities of the tree are its expressive and oracular powers, its usefulness in building foundations and its inner heat. It is also a symbol of sovereignty.

Divinatory message: alder

The alder draws your attention to the foundations of the matter in hand. It may be that the situation in question has arisen from some feature of the institutions, relationships or principles that form the framework of our lives. If so it is appropriate now to question these foundations. Are they supportive enough? Do they constrain you too much? Perhaps you need to consider your own principles. Are you having to compromise these too much or are they too idealized for other people to live up to? There is a reminder here that in many ways we are products of our social conditioning. Yet this conditioning can be questioned.

However it might be that there is a need to build foundations up rather than question them. Our lives need structure and security. Perhaps it is time for you to accept the need to make a commitment or to take on responsibility, to become the sovereign of your own life? It can sometimes be difficult to accept that other people rely on us, we doubt our ability to shoulder the burden. If you are worried by the demands put upon you by others then the Alder says to you that you do indeed have the strength to provide the support that the people around you need.

Another quality of the tree is its expressive power. It bleeds when cut, showing its feelings. Its wood makes pipes with a sweet sounding whistle and its associations with Bran connect it to oracular wisdom. The tree lives near water, the element symbolically associated with the emotions. Its message is therefore connected to the expression of feelings, intuitions or prophecies.

This may mean one of two things to you:

It may point to a prophecy of prior-warning that you have failed to heed or it may mean that you are not listening to your own feelings.

On the other hand the tree may be encouraging you to indulge in your expressive power. Is there something that you need to communicate. Have you some advice or a warning for someone that you are reluctant to give them?

Are you failing to state your needs? Or perhaps you have some creativity within you that you are not giving expression to?

In either case the alder counsels you to listen to your inner voice and trust your feelings.

A creative period may be before you. This could involve you laying the foundations for some future work.

Since alder is the tree of divination it may be that this tree stave is pointing, with self-reference, to trees and tree divination. If your question asked for guidance about where to turn to then the answer from the trees was: 'here we are'.

Apple

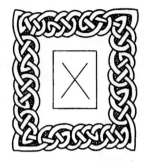

Latin Name: *Pyrus malus*
Ogham Name: Quert

With its health giving fruit and its heartening blossom the Apple tree is intimately bound up with the seasons of our life. In today's global economy all kinds of fruit and vegetable can be bought all year round and this undoubtedly helps to keep us healthy. Even so we have become more detached from the seasons because of it. Most town dwellers have little sense of harvest time or of the practical or spiritual meaning of the midwinter feast. In losing this connection with the seasons people's lives have become a grey procession of days punctuated by their holidays. 'Holiday' once meant 'holy day' but to many it now means no more than an escape from the workplace.

Modern pagans still celebrate the seasonal festivals of Yule, Beltane, Lammas and Samhain and commemorate the sun's progression from equinox through solstice back to equinox. For them the Apple retains its magical symbolism. At Beltane Apple blossom is a potent symbol of spring. At Samhain the Apple is a symbol of the death of the old year and the promise of the new.

An apple is a wholesome food that sustains life, and within itself it contains the seeds of new life. Hence a round shining apple is the perfect symbol of the ever turning wheel of the year, a gift of the Triple Goddess of the Cycle of Rebirth.

This is the tree of Iduna, the goddess of eternal youth and so is a symbol of eternal life. This symbolism repeats itself across Europe. Avalon, in Somerset, was the sacred Isle of Apples where life was renewed. Indeed many travellers to Glastonbury today still perceive the sacred energy of the area.

In myth there is a recurrent image of a Goddess who confers life with the gift of fruit from an Apple tree. The Norse Goddess Iduna kept the Gods alive with her magic apples. Hera fed the Gods with apples from the tree of life. The Old Testament provides a debased version of this myth where Eve, stripped of her Goddess status tempts Adam with an Apple. This example of how myth was distorted to serve patriarchal authority does however throw light on the connection between the apple and eternal life.

The apple is a symbol of sexuality and for this reason is also a symbol of Aphrodite, Goddess of love. The hidden message of these myths is that sacred sexuality is the key to health and long life, something that the Tantric Buddhists of the East have known for thousands of years. The proverb 'an apple a day keeps the doctor away' is a hint that regular healthy sexual intercourse is a sure way to fitness and health.

The apple has long been associated with healing and immortality. King Arthur was taken to the Isle of Apples to heal his battle wounds. In Irish myth a sacred apple branch, called the 'Craebh Civil', made joy inspiring music which healed the sick. The Goddess Diana was often portrayed carrying an apple-bough, representing her immortality.

In addition to Diana, the apple was sacred to a variety of goddesses of love and life including Aphrodite, Venus, Freia, Frigga and Olwen. When an apple is cut across its middle a five pointed star is revealed. This star, the pentagram, is also a symbol of the goddess of life. It represents the five stations of life: conception, birth, life, death and reincarnation; also

39

the five senses and the five elements that are required for life: earth, air, fire, water and spirit.

The Bach apple flower remedy is for those people who have a feeling of uncleanness. This is explained by the above, for undoubtedly it is sexual guilt that is the cause of the unclean feeling.

Apples are a highly nutritious food, containing easily digested fruit sugars, vitamins and minerals. Herbally they aid digestion. They even clean the teeth. And they make that splendid drink, Cider.

Apples are used in many love spells. Eat an apple whole, saving just the pips. An odd number foretells a marriage, an even number means that none is imminent.

Stuck with cloves an apple is a highly fragrant room freshener.

In Somerset the allocation of land to commoners was done by lot using apples marked to indicate a plot of common land. In this respect the apple can signify choice and in particular the fact that the choices we make can never have a certain outcome.

As if to remind us that life is an ever turning wheel the apple is not only a symbol of life but also a symbol of death. The 'pomegranate' eaten by Persephone that signalled her commitment to stay with Hades for half of each year was in fact an apple. Pomegranate means 'many seeded apple'. Traditions of apple bobbing at hallowe'en also reflect the association of the apple with the realms beyond life. The message here is clear: death is not a final end but a life beyond life, just as from the fallen apple comes the seeds of a new tree. The story of Snow White captures this message well: Snow White (the Goddess of Summer) eats the apple and falls into a death like sleep. Yet she awakes again, touched by the kiss of a prince (the Sun), who dislodged the apple from her mouth.

The qualities of the tree are: sexual love, longevity, cleansing and the underworld. It is the 'tree of love' and a symbol of the goddess of love and of life.

Divinatory message: Apple

The apple is a symbol of earthly desires. This tree is telling you to be open to your desires. Live life to the full.

Sexuality is the basis of life. If it harms no one then free yourself of any guilt and shame associated with your sexuality and indulge it. As Freud pointed out many physical illnesses are in fact caused by neuroses arising out of sexual repression. The apple is a reminder that sexuality is a gift of the Goddess of Life and can be a way to honour her.

Guilt is the most destructive and repressive of emotions. The guilt laden upon Eve has been used for centuries to control and demean the vital energy of women. It is time to relieve Eve from the burden of her guilt. Think about how you are controlled by guilt. Are you allowing yourself to be exploited for fear of the guilt that comes from refusing to meet the demands of other people?

In many cases women are brought up to believe that they are responsible for nurturing and taking care of everyone around them. Hence if someone is unhappy women tend to feel responsible. Yet it is unrealistic to expect people to have so much responsibility for how other people are feeling. If you can relate this to yourself then you must recognise that your own needs are as important as other people's. Many women will find this hard to accept. You may even find it hard to identify what your own needs are. If this is the case then it is time to start to nurture yourself and to find and protect your own boundaries. This will not be easy but it is your choice and your right. Make a connection with your higher self through your own spirituality. Meditation can be a valuable place to start from and there are many very empowering books available teaching meditation. When you have made that connection then give yourself permission to draw on the energy of the universe and learn to be assertive, to say 'No' when it is appropriate and 'Yes' when it is.

For men the challenge is just as important. Men need to question the expectations that they have of women and the demands that they make of them. To be truly supportive they need to become aware of the ways in which they feed into the exploitation of women. Many men will have been socialised into having unrealistic expectations about the domestic and emotional support that women should give. Men also have to learn to mother themselves, their partners and their children.

It may also be time to give more thought to your physical health. How are you feeding your body? Remember that you are what you eat. Use all of your senses to choose your food. Eat what looks wholesome. When faced with a choice of food use your sense of smell to decide what you want to eat.

Life is the greatest of gifts. We should honour the divine by living our life to the full. The apple can represent a choice. Every moment of our lives we are faced with the choice of how to live it. This is all too often forgotten and the language that we use reflects and reinforces our sense of powerlessness. Next time you hear yourself saying something like: "So and so is making me sad", change the words around and say: "I am choosing to feel sad about so and so". Admit that you have the option to feel differently.

Ash

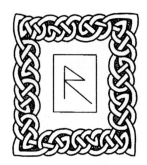

Latin name: *Fraxinus Excelsior*
Ogham Name: Nuin

This handsome tree is tall and substantial with long slender branches. It has several characteristic features: its silvery grey bark, the matt black buds, the feathery compound leaves and the bunches of 'Ash-keys' which spin delightfully to the ground like helicopters.

The tree grows quickly, becoming mature after only 40 to 50 years. The elasticity of its timber is ideal for tool making. It has traditionally been used for arrows, spears, oars, carriage shafts, cart wheels, tool handles, ladders, walking sticks and even aeroplanes. It is appropriate that many of these relate to travel for, as we shall see, the tree is symbolic of travel.

Various legends illustrate the connection of the Ash with travel. The handle of witches broomsticks are made of ash to enable speedy travel in the air and across waters. The Norse god Odin used the tree as his horse. This tree was called 'Yggdrasil' which means 'Odin's magic steed'. Sailors used to carry small ash carvings as a protection against drowning.

Several cultures share the legend that humans were made from the Ash. In Nordic traditions the first man, Askr, was made from an ash log. This may have arisen from the attraction that lightning has for the tree which demonstrates its connection to the energy of the Gods.

The dominant image from the mythologies associated with the Ash is that of the World Tree which links the realms of Gods, Humans and the Dead. The Ash facilitates travel between these worlds. The lightning bolt also connects these worlds, coming from the heavens down to earth and then going into the underworld. In the Jewish mystical system known as Cabbalism the 'Tree of Life' is a diagram that maps all of existence. In this diagram the spirit of creation is seen as travelling down the tree in the shape of a lightning flash.

Each 'sphere' of the tree represents the creation of ever more physical layers of reality. The numbering of these spheres follows the order of their creation and creates the pattern of a lightning bolt.

Ash is often associated with the number three. In Norse mythology the World Tree had three huge roots. One went into the underground spring of Urd (Earth) where the Norns lived, dispensing justice and deciding the fates of men and women. This was also the role of the Greek Goddess Nemesis, who carried an Ash branch as a symbol of justice.

The second root reached the well of Mimir in the land of the frost giants. This well is the source of all wisdom. It was for this wisdom that the God Odin hung himself from the Ash tree for 9 nights (3 times 3).

The third root went to Niflhelm, the underworld ruled by the Goddess Hel. The Ash tree has been used to represent the journey to and return from the underworld, hence the Ash is also associated with rebirth and healing.

The qualities of the Ash tree are travel, especially speedy travel, wisdom obtained through travel, fate, the journey to the underworld and rebirth. It is intimately connected with the number three.

Divinatory message: Ash

Ash is connected to the number three. Three is the number of the dialectical process. In philosophy this is the theory that all development proceeds through a process of contradiction and the resolution of that contradiction. This is regarded as a fundamental law of nature and can be used to explain the development of ideas, of political systems and even of life itself. For example in developing a new idea someone may start by rejecting an established theory. Having two opposite viewpoints to consider they then will discover a middle ground, a synthesis which is closer to the truth than either the original theory or its antithesis.

It can be seen that a journey and return is involved here, since the antithesis is a journey away from the thesis, and the syntheses is a return to the original thesis but with something added. Likewise the hero who travels to the underworld always returns with something more than when they set out. The dialectical process is the essence of psychotherapy and counselling, where the client takes a journey into hidden aspects of themselves and returns with a deeper understanding of themself.

The Tree Of Life

Sphere
1	=	The world of pure spirit
2	=	The matrix of creation
3	=	The act of creation
4	=	Creation of Space
5	=	Creation of Time
6	=	Self-awareness, the soul
7	=	Feelings
8	=	Thoughts
9	=	The subconscious, the astral
10	=	The world of physical sensations

Sometimes conflict and contradiction are just what we need in our life. All relationships have arguments but if something is learned in those arguments, if new perspective is obtained, then the arguments are often worth having. Yet when we argue we all too often get locked into defending our own position and try to prove that we are in the right. Be brave and go on a journey: try to see things from the other person's point of view for a few minutes. Let go of your dogged attachment to being in the right. In a day or so you will have forgotten all about it anyway. Instead try to discover the lesson in this for both of you.

Hence the message of the Ash tree is that you must be prepared to consider a point of view which is different to, even the opposite of, what you believe at the moment. The way forward for you is to synthesise the truthful elements of these opposite viewpoints. You must explore and assimilate.

The Ash may also represent travel between different places, people or cultures and the bringing back of new knowledge from that journey.

As a symbol of justice and fate the Ash may be forcing you to face up to the consequences of your actions or way of being. You have been given this life to learn a certain lesson and grow from that. This is your karma. If you try to avoid this lesson then fate, The Norns, will find you and challenge you. If, however, you face this lesson and embrace the dialectical process then you can look forward to a rebirth into greater wholeness.

Aspen

Latin name: *Populus tremula*
Ogham name: Eoda

The aspen has very round leaves which flutter madly with the slightest breeze. This has led to its being known as the 'shiver tree' or 'shaking ash'. The constant shaking of the leaves enables the tree to shake off any water lying on the leaves which it then absorbs.

This 'shivering' quality led to the belief that Aspen had the power to heal fevers, which in medieval times were known as 'the ague'. A lock of the patient's hair was pinned to the trunk and the following spell was said:

> 'Aspen tree, I pray to thee
> Shake and shiver instead of me'.

The Bach flower remedy is for psychological fears of an unknown origin, fear of sleep and of dreams and fears associated with death and religion. It is undoubtedly indicated for people who 'shake' with fear.

The Celts used the wood to make protective shields which would have had the magic effect of dispelling their fear in battle.

The Greek for aspen is 'Aspis' which also means shield.

In Ireland coffin makers used a measuring rod made of Aspen to measure corpses to fit the coffin and to measure the coffin

49

to fit the grave. It has been speculated that this was to ease the fears of the dead in their journey to the underworld as it is a symbol that death would be followed by resurrection.

Several legends indicate that the tree has a connection to communication.

The whispering sound made by the shaking of the leaves was said to be a message from the tree. The tree shook because it had very sensitive hearing. Placing an aspen leaf under the tongue would bring eloquence. Druids could hear the voice of the future by listening to the wind whispering through the trees leaves.

The qualities of the tree are: A shield that prevents fear and a quiet whispered message.

Divinatory message: Aspen

Our higher self has a quiet voice that we rarely hear when our minds are full of the clamour of everyday life. The art of meditation is to attain the balance and tranquillity of the aspen tree. We can then enjoy an enhanced sensitivity and hear the quiet whisper of the wind in the trees and the even quieter whisper of our deepest truth.

The aspen may be suggesting that if you are trying to get a message accross then you may be more successful if you communicate with quiet confidence rather than by shouting and screaming.

Fear limits our senses and freezes our ability to think. As it says in Frank Herbert's novel *Dune*: "Fear is the mind killer. Fear is the little-death that brings total oblivion". In a truly perilous situation fear is a vital survival instinct ensuring that the mind focuses on escape. Yet in the modern world many people live with fear as a matter of course: fear of losing their jobs, fear of what people might think of them, fear of being alone, fear of failure, fear of success. These fears are ingrained in us by a socialisation process designed to create a society that conforms and obeys. The aspen hints at the promise of living without fear and freeing the mind from its constraints.

Look at the fears that inhibit your life. What are your ambitions? What fears prevent you from persuing them? Are these fears a reality? What would happen if they came true?

Life can be a risky business. There is only one sure way to avoid failure and that is to never attempt anything! We should not fear failure, we should be grateful to it for it is one of life's greatest teachers. Successful people take risks. Sometimes they fail, sometimes they succeed but they always learn.

Beech

Latin name: *Fagus sylvatica*
Ogham name: Phogos, meaning bright
white light

This impressive, majestic tree is a glory all year round. In winter its smooth grey trunk is revealed. It looks like elephant skin. Its branches and twigs against the sky resemble a network of fine veins. As summer comes the tree fills with a mass of leaves, whose colour matures as the months pass. In spring they are yellow-green, in summer an oily dark green and in autumn a blaze of rich browns and copper hues.

In hot dry summers the Beech flowers and produces nuts known as beechmast which provides abundant and nutritious food for woodland creatures. The tree also improves the fertility of the soil around it and its enormous spreading crown provides a home for a wealth of bird and insect life.

However despite its size Beech is a sensitive tree. Its cambium layer is near to the surface of its bark, making it susceptible to injury. It is also very sensitive to light and soaks up sunlight energy.

Beech wood was used for writing tablets. These were used in the construction of the first books. Beech is especially suited to the making of magic talismans. Beech is the tree of the written word and is a guardian of past knowledge and wisdom.

53

Herbally Beech is used to treat a range of skin diseases, and homeopathically for conditions associated with nervous tension. Hence the sensitivity of the tree provides a remedy for illnesses brought on by over sensitivity.

The qualities of the tree are beauty, sensitivity and giving of nutrition. These qualities are summed up well by its title 'Mother of the Woods'.

Divinatory message: Beech

This tree tells you to exploit your sensitive faculties. The answer to the question facing you will come from a communication from another realm. This may be the past or the future, from a dream or from a passing remark, from a voice within you or from a friend. The message is there - you have to be sensitive enough to recognise it.

The Beech reminds you that you have a storehouse of knowledge and wisdom in your memories. Contemplate past events that are shaping your present (and your future). Do you need to heal the pain of these events? Do you need to draw strength from the well of your memories? Are you repeating behaviour patterns from your past? It is time to connect with this guidance from your past.

The tree also asks you to consider who and what needs your protective nurturing. This is a time to be sensitive to the messages around you. Sometimes people fail to articulate their real needs but communicate those needs more subtly. Look behind the words and actions of the people around you and try to pick up a feeling for what they are asking for. This is particularly important with children, who are often unable to express their needs verbally. A child's 'naughty' behaviour may well be their attempt to ask for attention or to express some insecurity.

Beech, being a synonym in Celtic languages for 'literature' may also indicate that you need to look in books to find the information that you are looking for.

Silver Birch

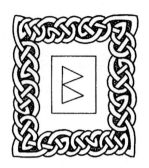

Latin Name: *Betula pendula*
Ogham name: Beith, meaning
 'shining one' or 'bright'
Rune: Berkana, meaning growth

The graceful delicacy of the Birch belies its toughness. The tree's silvery trunk rises straight like a column from which its branches and twigs elegantly hang. Yet the tree is very hardy and thrives in places where more sturdy trees would fail to grow such as Greenland, Iceland and Siberia. The birch is therefore the most feminine of trees exemplifying both delicate beauty and deep inner strength. The birch is one of the first trees to grow on clear land and so has been named the 'initiator of woods'.

In both sunlight and moonlight the Silver Birch is enchanting. To Coleridge it was the 'Lady of the Woods'. It gives an impression of ethereal lightness and truly seems to be from the lands of elphin.

The tree is associated with the Goddess at springtime. It is one of the first trees to come into leaf...and to come into life. Both the Anglo-Saxon Goddess of spring Eostre and the Norse Goddess of fertility Frigga were associated with the tree. Birch woods were a favourite place for the Mayday customs where young lovers would conjure the awakening of the earth.

Birch was used in spells of purification and protection since the tree's freshness was thought to ward off negative and outworn influences. The tree was used in spells to bestow

57

fertility. These fertility spells were worked on a range of creatures including cattle and newly wed couples.

Birch wood is the traditional wood for cradles and was thought to protect infants from evil spirits. Hanging birch branches in the home is said to bring good luck and dispel harmful spirits. The custom of 'Birching' offenders has more to do with the power of Birch to drive out evil spirits than any theory about deterrent effects. Likewise witches use their birch twig brooms to 'sweep' away any unwanted negative energies before beginning a ritual. Knotty balls of twigs called burrels grow in the branches of Birch trees when the tree overproduces twig growth to protect itself from fungal or insect attack. These are known as 'witches brooms' or 'witches knots', confirming the association of the tree with witches. These 'witches' were in fact the people who maintained a devotion to the Anglo-Saxon Goddesses and Gods after Christianisation. They would have continued traditions and rituals near to the Birch and hence the tree became associated with 'witches'.

The Anglo-Saxon rune poem describes Birch thus: 'Splendid are its branches and gloriously adorned, its lofty crown reaching the sky'. The rune Beorc (also known as Berkana) shares these associations with spring and purification. It indicates new growth and counsels you to clear and purify the ground in preparation for this growth. When starting a new project it advises you to examine your motives and ensure that they are pure. The ritual of spring cleaning is a sign that there is an instinctive knowledge that this time of new growth is the appropriate time to clear away the old and purify our houses.

Birch sap is a sweet spring tonic. It is known as 'birch water'. It is cleansing for the skin, flushes away kidney stones and is a freshening mouthwash.

The qualities of this tree are purification, new growth and spring cleaning.

Divinatory message: Birch

The message of this tree is appropriately clear and simple. New growth is at hand. It is time to clear away unhygenic conditions and negative energies to ensure that the growth will be healthy. It is time to drive away the spirit of the old and welcome the new.

In early spring it often feels as if winter is still here. Likewise when the fruitful energy of the Birch begins to take hold you may still feel very stagnant. If you feel stuck in a rut then start to look for the signs of new growth that are there in your life. Under the fallen leaves of your old habits and routines will lie the first shoots of fresh new ideas and projects. To foster these new shoots it is worthwhile clearing away the dead leaves and letting some light in. Examine your life for any outworn habits and review the value of any activities that you are not finding fulfilling.

Beginnings are a time of vigour and energy. There is a danger that this energy may be dissipated too quickly if it is not used efficiently. At the beginning of any project it is well worth putting some time aside to make a plan of what needs to be done and how. A little thought put into planning at this stage will repay itself many times over as the project unfolds.

When new growth starts small variations in conditions can have a dramatic effect on the final result. For this reason it is vital that you have the right attitude towards any new project. Examine your motivations. What are you really trying to get out of the project? Is this the most efficient way to get what you want or would a more direct approach be more honest and productive? Are you going along with this project to please someone else? If you can be clear in your mind that

60

your motives are pure then your energy and motivation will not be distracted from its goal.

In Wales girls gave a piece of birch twig to their desired lovers. This gift from the tree of inception implied: "you may begin". If you have drawn the birch stave then the message is the same: it is time to make the first move.

Blackthorn

Latin name: *Prunus spinosa*
Ogham name: Straif

The blackthorn has very crooked dark twigs bearing viciously sharp spines. It blossoms in early spring (before the hawthorn) in a mass of white flowers. Its fruit are the dark purple 'Sloes' which are used to make Sloe Gin.

The tree is an excellent hedge plant due to its ability to grow dense clusters of spiny branches. The thorns can draw copious quantities of blood and the wounds often turn septic. Blackthorn thorns are used for harmful spells. The long hard sharp thorns were also used to prick people with poison. In Ireland these were called 'Bor an Suan' which means 'Pins of slumber'.

A blackthorn staff was the badge of the village 'wise woman' and 'cunning man'. These were people whose understanding of herbalism, healing, midwifery and psychology made them a vital resource in the community. Their resourcefulness and independent natures were not, however, of liking to either the church or the Lord of the Manor. Village healers, often independent and strong minded women, came to be labelled 'witches' and persecuted mercilessly. To add insult to injury the pyres used to burn the 'witches' often contained blackthorn wood, the sacred tree of the witch.

The Irish cudgel known as the 'shillelagh' was made from Blackthorn. Blackthorn staffs and wands are used for projecting powerful blasts of psychic energy ('blasting').

63

Although this energy can and should be used positively for sending healing it is likely that the rural 'witch' would sometimes use the threat of it as a protection from harassment. Even so, stories of witches causing harm and miscarriages by using their 'black rods' were in most cases due to misogynistic prejudice and persecution.

Blackthorn is also powerful when used for fertility magic. Like Hawthorn, its musky scent is highly erotic. It was bound with Hawthorn to make crowns for Maypoles. In Worcester at New Year a Blackthorn garland was burned and the ashes scattered on the fields to encourage the fertility of the soil. In the North of England a globe was constructed from Blackthorn branches and this was carried around the apple trees to promote new growth and fertility.

The tree has also been seen as highly protective. In France the tree is known as 'La Mere du Bois' which means the mother of the woods. In an Irish legend a hero pursued by a giant threw a blackthorn twig behind him. This twig quickly grew into a dense wood of thorns and halted the giant. This story may be based on another of the magical uses of the plant: that of 'binding' malevolent energies so that they can cause no harm.

The thorns of the tree were used to pierce waxen effigies of people ('poppets'). The common assumption is that the purpose of piercing a wax image is to cause a corresponding pain in the person that the image represented. This is however only partially true. In many instances such spells were done to alleviate pain and bring about cures. In other instances the spell could bring about love and heal relationships. However it must be said that when a Blackthorn thorn was used for piercing a poppet the intention of the spell was probably malevolent.

The Homeopathic remedy is used for shooting, piercing pains such as neuralgia.

The qualities of the tree are: Projective and protective magic.

Divinatory message: Blackthorn

The Blackthorn tolerates no messing. It is a conductor of very powerful energies. If this tree draws you then you must be prepared to treat it with the highest respect. The message may be that there is something in your life which you are not treating with sufficient importance. It may be necessary to give more energy to this thing or it may be necessary to limit its effect. In either case you must not ignore it.

It may now be time for you to face up to something that you have been avoiding. If so you will know by now that this thing is not going to go away. In these circumstances the Blackthorn's protective magic reassures you that it is safe to confront the issue for the time is now right.

The blackthorn raises the possibility that you are the victim of psychological or psychic attack. Like all forms of bullying this occurs when someone plays on the weakness, fears or disadvantages of their victim. That it is done from a deep sense of insecurity and powerlessness is rarely a solace to the victim of such attack.

Psychic attack happens when someone directs negative energy to you. This can be done intentionally but often happens unintentionally when someone harbours resentment against you. You may feel agitated and distressed for no reason or start to feel headaches or other pains. If this is the case you must take measures to protect yourself. This is quite easy. Imagine a cloak of white or golden light surrounding your body like a shell. Any negative energy sent to you will be reflected away from you and will rebound upon the sender. In addition ask your guardian spirits to watch over you and to ensure that your protective cloak is maintained, especially while you sleep.

Psychological attack can be harder to deal with. There are a number of possible ways to deal with it. Circumstances will determine which are appropriate. It can sometimes be helpful to confront the bully with the effects of what they are doing. Sometimes people are unaware of how hurtful their comments can be. At times it may be necessary to inform a third party. When sexual harassment occurs at work this should be done formally and as soon as possible. In some circumstances the best way to deal with psychological attack is to avoid the bully. As long as this does not prevent you from being where you wish to be then this should not be construed as running away.

The above comments also apply to physical abuse. These few remarks only touch on what is a difficult and destructive problem but it must be said that bullying should never be tolerated, a solution to it should always be found.

One final word. If you yourself are guilty of psychically or psychologically attacking someone then consider the law of 'threefold' return. Know that any negative energy that you send out will return to you many times over.

Elðer

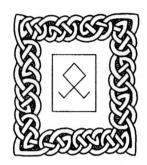

Latin name: *Sambucus nigra*
Ogham name: Ruis

This broadly crowned deciduous shrub blossoms into a mass of creamy white flowers to herald the start of summer. Later in the year it is hung with heavy bunches of black berries. The wood is light and papery and the young shoots can be easily hollowed out to make whistles and pop-guns. The tree grows rampantly, especially on chalky soil.

The name 'Elder' derives from the Anglo-Saxon '*Êld*' which means 'fire'. It has been suggested that this is due to the fact that the hollowed out stalks of the tree were used to blow air to stoke fires.

In pagan times the Elder was regarded as a very sacred tree. This is partly explained by the numerous medicinal uses that it can be put to. However the magical atmosphere of the tree cannot be denied. Its stooped and twisting branches always seem to set the tree apart, whether full of white flowers in summer, hanging with black berries in the autumn or bare and wizened in winter.

The Elder was revered as being very magical. It was known as Lady Elder and its magic was said to stem from the 'Elder Mother', a spirit who dwelt in the tree. In Germanic countries she was called 'Hylde-Moer'. Her spirit was said to haunt those people who cut elder wood without asking her permission. Babies who slept in cots made of elder wood were said to be taunted by the pinching of this vengeful spirit.

67

Mrs Grieve, in her herbal, quotes the words used by woods-men before cutting elder: "Lady Ellhorn, give me some of thy wood and I will give thee some of mine when it grows in the forest". This shows an appreciation of one of the principles of Karma: we always have to pay later for what we take now.

When Christianity eradicated pagan customs the elder tree came in for particular attack. The tree was slandered as being evil and it was said that the trees were witches in disguise. The cross upon which Jesus was executed was said to be made of Elder wood and Judas was said to have hung himself upon an elder tree. These anachronistic stories are clearly attempts to blacken the image of a tree that was held in great reverence by the pagan people. Even so the tree's healing and magical qualities were not forgotten and it has continued to have a special place in the lives of country people.

The tree has the ability to regenerate itself from damaged branches. For this reason it has been called the tree of regeneration.

Pipes made from Elder stalks are said to conjure up spirits. It is believed that if you sleep under the tree on Midsummer's Eve you will see the King and Queen of Faerie and their wonderful land. The atmosphere of the tree is indeed narcotic and sleep inducing.

The tree is highly medicinal. David Hoffman in "*The New Holistic Herbal*", p197 writes:

"*The elder tree is a veritable medicine chest in itself. The leaves are used primarily for bruises, sprains, wounds and chilblains. It has been reported that Elder leaves may be useful in an ointment for tumours. Elder flowers are ideal for the treatment of colds and influenza. They are indicated in any catarrhal inflammation of the upper respiratory tract such as hayfever and sinusitis. Catarrhal deafness responds well to*

Elder flowers. Elder berries have similar properties to the flowers with the addition of their usefulness in rheumatism".

A look at any herbal will reveal more of the many beneficial properties of the tree. The homeopathic remedy is used for ailments arising from fright and where frightening images occur in dreams and when closing the eyes (an interesting symptom given the reputation of the tree to conjure up spirits).

Elder is not only healing for humans but also benefits the fields in which it grows. Farmers believed that elder in their hedgerows was good for their livestock and they have used the leaves of the tree to ward off vermin and insects.

The tree has associations with death. In Germany it is called Holunder, linking it with Hel, the Goddess of death. King William Rufus was said to have been killed by an arrow shot by an archer posted under an elder tree. This implies that the tree had some symbolic or ritual connection with death. This was possibility an indication that the 'Elder Mother' was a version of the Crone aspect of the Triple Goddess. The Crone is the Goddess of death, healing, magic and regeneration: all attributes of this tree. In Norse mythology the Goddess Freya chose an elder as her home.

The other aspects of the Triple Goddess also have their sacred trees. The maiden aspect of the Goddess, bringing inspiration and new growth is seen in the Apple, Silver Birch and Pine. The mother aspect, representing fruition and nurturing is personified by the Beech, Lime and Rowan. The crone aspect is seen in the Elder, Yew and Willow. None of these attributions should be seen as being fixed. The beauty of trees is that they each personify all the seasons and all aspects of divinity as they follow the cycle of the year.

The keywords for this tree correspond to the Crone aspect of the Triple Goddess: magic, healing, regeneration and divination.

Divinatory message: Elder

The message of the 'Elder Mother' is never trivial. She demands a mature response to the challenge that life sets. This will mean that you must call upon all of your innate wisdom and see the problems or issues at hand from a holistic perspective. You may be being asked to put a selfish or one-sided interest to one side for the sake of the greater good.

A question of health may be at the root of things. If this is the case then you should consider the holistic implications of a lifestyle that makes many demands upon the body's physical and mental systems.

It has been said that the elder represents 'death in life'. In one sense this is a warning against stagnation and being in a rut. There is a need to let go of what is passing. This is holding you back. To get on with life you have to accept change. This may mean growing up. Growing up may require you to review and challenge the values that you have inherited from your social conditioning.

The Elder Mother also serves as a reminder that we are all subject to the laws of Karma. What we take in one life we will give back in another. What we give in this life will be returned to us in another. So even when life is hard we must live it as well we can for, as it says in psalm 126, they that sow in tears shall reap in joy.

If you have been drawn to the Elder then there is a good chance that you are being led towards the path of natural magic, healing or divination. The Crone Goddess is also the Goddess of magic and wisdom. Remain open to Her influence and look out for signs that will lead you towards the development of these skills. Allow yourself to feel the healing energy in your hands. Hold your hands to your heart and feel the peace and warmth that comes from them. If you have an interest in herbalism then the Elder is strongly encouraging you to pursue it.

Elm

Latin Name: *Ulmus campestris*
Ogham name: Ailm

This tall and heavily crowned tree was once a defining feature of the English countryside. The paintings of Constable captured this tree in its glory. Tragically Dutch Elm disease has killed all of the old Elms. The disease now limits the life of the tree to 30 years, at which age it becomes vulnerable to attack by the beetle which carries the disease.

The Elm is a tree of femininity. In Norse creation myths the first woman, 'Embla', came from the Elm. Kipling wrote: 'Ailim be the lady's tree; burn it not or cursed ye'll be'. In Latin countries the Elm was taken to be a symbol of the Triple Goddess Diana, the consort of the Vine, symbol of the God Bacchus. Elms were often planted in vineyards to provide a framework for the vines to grow on. Elm and Vine entwined portrayed the balance of the divine couple.

Elm is a tree of purification. It used to be used to make soap and skin cleansers. Culpepper wrote that "the water that is found in bladders on the leaves is very effectual to cleanse the skin and make it fair". As a Bach flower remedy the Elm is recommended to people who shoulder the burdens of responsibility and sometimes get overwhelmed by the magnitude of their tasks.

In legend and use Elm is connected to death. Elm wood was commonly used to make coffins. The tree was also connected to ancient burial mounds and the Elfin people which were

73

said to live within them. Over the past half century Elm disease has spread havoc among the trees. It is a cruel coincidence that this period has also seen the mechanisation of farming and the thoughtless destruction of many ancient earthworks and barrows.

So at the start of the new millennium the Elm seems to represent that which has been lost in this industrial age. The great old elm trees which were once an integral part of the landscape have died. Yet much of that landscape itself has gone forever, torn up and sterilised by 'scientific' farming methods, open cast mining and road building schemes.

Farmers have used the Elm for centuries as a guide to changes within nature. Times for the planting and harvesting of the Barley crop were based on the appearance and growth of the leaves. An early fall of the leaves was taken as a warning that there would be some illness in the cattle herd. That it was a reliable indicator of such things poses the question of whether the Elm's destruction is an omen of impending ecological disaster.

The destruction caused by the ravages of Dutch Elm disease serves as a warning of the vulnerability of each species on the planet and a reminder that we often only realise the true value of things once they have been lost.

Keywords: purification, death, disease, destruction of the environment

Divinatory message: Elm

Some lessons are harder to learn than others. At the start of the 21st century the message of the Elm seems to be that we must become more aware of the massive destructive potential of small individual actions. A tiny beetle can destroy a species of tree, a farmer's desire to increase his profits can lead to the destruction of our heritage, the desire to drive a car can lead to the tearing up of massive strips of land and forest to build new roads.

This process can be seen on an individual level as well. Bad habits can lead to bad health and death. We know how smoking cigarettes can lead to the destruction of the lungs or how eating fatty foods clogs up the arteries. What we are less aware of is how our psychological habits build up over the years to wear down our spirit. Every time we say something critical we become more critical in ourselves. Over the years these thoughtless remarks can turn us into an embittered old person. Every time we compromise our principles we lose something of ourselves. Watch out for any small bad habits that you may have, any negative attitudes and become aware of their destructive effect.

The message of the elm for you may be at one of many levels. The challenge facing you may be as global as fighting the destruction of the environment or as personal as the need to give up smoking or wake up each day with a smile. Whatever the scope of the challenge one thing will be clear: it will require the resolution to be constantly aware of the consequences of every small action. Yet do not despair for, as it says in the Tao Te Ching:

> If you start with your own true self
> The power of the small builds up in you
> Like a well that never fails
> And then nothing can stop you.

The power of the small should never be underestimated. It is the power in the water of streams which can cut great canyons through the earth. It is the power of the seed, which can grow into a great tree. It is the power of the fertilised egg, which in the womb of a woman's body develops at an astonishing rate. This is feminine power, Goddess power and we all have it within us, Woman or Man. In being lead to the Elm you are reminded of this. No matter how difficult, massive or seemingly impossible the task before you know that it can be achieved through gentle perseverance.

Hawthorn

Latin name: *Cratagus oxyacantha*
Ogham name: Huathe

Hawthorn is usually seen as a dense shrub, a feature of many hedges. However it can grow into a well defined tree of up to 30ft. Indeed there is such a tree in my garden, and this throbs with bird life all year round. The mass of white blossom appearing after Beltane (May Day) give the tree its other common names: 'May' or 'Whitethorn'. Hawthorn can live for hundreds of years, developing gnarled twisted trunks full of the hardy character of old age.

The tree is intimately connected to marriage and fertility. Celtic pagans held their marriage ceremonies at Beltane when the Hawthorn is full of erotically scented white blossom. Even after a thousand years of church suppression of the heritage and customs of the people the use of confetti at weddings hints at folk memories of the aphrodisiac power of the musky sensual odour of the May blossom. The hawthorn symbolises the forces of sexual attraction and the physical manifestations of this such as body language and phero-mones.

Appropriately for a plant associated with love, Hawthorn is a heart tonic, both in herbal and homeopathic doses. Country folk know that chewing the leaves is a good way to relieve hunger. The leaves are often known as 'bread and cheese'. A refreshing tea can also be made from the leaves.

Despite its erotic power, which as Chaucer wrote 'fills full the wanton eye with May's delight', there is an ambivalent attitude towards the tree. Some consider it unlucky and refuse to have it in the house, in particular during the winter months. This ambivalence is explained by the fact that the tree is sacred to the White Goddess, who is not only the maiden of spring but also the death bringing crone of winter. The Goddess of Spring, whom the Celts called 'Bride' is evoked in images of the wedding bride and the tree in blossom. The Goddess of Winter, the Crone, is evoked by images of the widow cloaked in black and the bare tree with its gnarled bark and spiny thorns.

A further association between the Hawthorn and the Crone Goddess can be seen in the Greek Goddess Maia, a harsh goddess of wisdom and the winds who derived from the Hawthorn Goddess, Cardia. 'Maia' means 'Grandmother'.

The belief that it is unlucky to marry in the month of May derives from the Romans. During May they performed purification ceremonies and abstained from sexual inter-course. The Celts made a much lustier use of the energies of May.

Hawthorn's reputation as a symbol of protection undoubtedly arises from its stout self-protection. Its spiky thorns form a formidable barrier and some of those who have ignored the warning of these and attempted to cut through the tough wood have reputedly been blinded by flying splinters. Beware of even cutting a branch from a Hawthorn tree for ill luck is said to follow. This theme of self-protection is reflected in the rune associated with the tree, called 'Thurisaz' or 'Thorn'. This rune is used to invoke protective powers. It is sacred to the god Thor. This may explain the reason why the tree is often planted near to houses to prevent damage from light-ning. As a runic oracle 'Thorn' counsels caution and contemplation.

In Ireland hawthorns often grow around sacred wells. It is customary to hang small pieces of cloth from their branches and make a wish. The wish was said to come true when the wind or other visitors removed the cloth from the branch.

The qualities of Hawthorn reflect the traditional qualities of the Triple Goddess: In spring time marriage and fertility; in summer nourishment and in winter protection and caution.

Divinatory message: Hawthorn

This tree urges you to contemplate the appropriateness of your action. There is a time and a place for everything. As it says in the Book of Ecclesiastes: 'To every thing there is a season, and a time to every purpose under the heaven: A time to be born, and a time to die; a time to plant, and a time to pluck up that which is planted; A time to kill, and a time to heal; a time to break down, and a time to build up; A time to weep, and a time to laugh; a time to mourn, and a time to dance...'

As you become aware of the changing of the seasons within your life, you can discover the activities that are appropriate to those seasons. A project may require the rapid growth of spring, the maturing of summer or it may be necessary to rest from the project as the earth rests in winter. If you learn to see the activities of your life in these terms you will be able to cope with our natural cycles of energy.

So whatever your question, ask yourself what your energy is like in relation to it. Is it wild and passionate? Then go forth and multiply. Take the bull by the horns. Is it steady and positive? If so there is a need to allow things to mature and grow. Is your energy for the question destructive? Perhaps it is time to harvest what you have obtained and move on. Or do you have no energy for the question? Maybe you need to let it rest for a while.

As individuals we have our own distinct rhythms and patterns of energy. Some people feel most energetic in the morning, some at night. Everyone has a favourite season. However you feel at the moment, ask yourself how much this is due to the time of day, month or year. Try to work with your natural rhythms. It can be very stressful for the body to be out of step with its biological clock.

On another level the Hawthorn represents our fundamental survival needs: fertility, nourishment and protection. If this tree has drawn you then its message is that you must ensure that you are giving priority to your basic needs. Your integrity may be at stake here and if so you must consider the following questions: Do you feel safe? Do you feel nourished? Do you feel able to grow? Remember that these are human rights and are your rights.

On a lighter note, the Hawthorn is the tree of loving partnerships and the heart. Love may be in the air.

Hazel

Latin name: *Corylus avellana*
Ogham name: Coll

Hazel is a large shrub with a dense cluster of long shoots rising from the ground. These stems are ideal for coppicing - the practise of cutting the tree at ground level and harvesting the many straight shoots that grow. Hazel grows quickly and the atmosphere around the Hazel tree is of fast-moving energy. Being close to a Hazel tree induces an anxious state in me which I have now as I write this.

The Hazel is the Celtic tree of knowledge and wisdom. In legend its nuts were eaten by the salmon of wisdom, a fish revered for the amazing feat of its annual return against strong river currents to its spawning ground. The nuts were also considered to be a food of the gods and could only be eaten by humans on ceremonial occasions.

In one Irish legend five Hazel nuts fell into a pool of water and were eaten by five salmon. From this pool five streams emerged, and the shells of the nuts each travelled down one of the five streams. This story is an allegory for the five senses, each of which carry information and knowledge to the brain. In a related legend nine nuts were eaten by a salmon. The nine spots on the salmon's skin are said to be a legacy of this. The number nine is the number of classical arts and sciences and again the Hazel and the salmon pool represent the sources of wisdom.

Hazel is sacred to the God Mercury. Mercury was the fleet footed messenger of the Gods, just as the planet Mercury is the fastest moving planet. The mercurial, snake like energy of the Hazel and the speed of its growth meant that it has been associated with Mercury from ancient times. Hence Hazel is the preferred wood for making magic wands, being the wood of the magician God.

The tree also has strong associations with water. It grows well in watery places and it is well known as a tool for water divining. It is also connected to water in a wider sense. To the ancients the element 'water' denoted not just H_2O but any material whose properties were liquid and could move in waves. The modern understanding of sound and light waves draws a connection between the Hazel and all forms of energy that moves in waves. Messages are energy in motion. The Hazel represents all such messages. Here again the link with Mercury can be seen. Words were his gift to humanity and now a thought can be sent across the world at the speed of light.

The swiftness with which words can carry a message can be both positive and negative. Words can be used for both useful communication and malicious gossip. In some myths the Hazel tree drips poisonous milk and is an abode of vultures and ravens. These stories of the 'dripping Hazel' challenge the notion that the gift of language has always been a benefit for humanity. Animals cannot speak but neither do they lie.

Hazel rods are used for dowsing. In medieval England the forked Hazel was not only used for divining hidden treasure and water but also for determining people's guilt.

To the Druids Hazel was the tree of inspiration. It was the 'poet's tree' and was carried as a symbol of rank by druids to whom poetry was a sacred way of connecting to the divine. The Hazel wand was said to guarantee the bearer a fair hearing in a dispute. These divinatory and inspirational uses of Hazel spring once again from its ability to seek out and connect with energy waves. Hazel allows you to 'tap' the lines of psychic energy that surround us and is even said to allow access to those parallel worlds that exist at a different level of vibration - the faerie lands.

The qualities of the tree are wisdom and inspiration gained from a connection with channels of energy.

Divinatory message: Hazel

The Hazel represents all sources of wisdom and knowledge. It points to the need to learn and understand the world around you and the need to express and share this creatively. An involvement with studying or teaching may be indicated.

The Hazel is the tree of divining - of revealing what is hidden. Its message warns that this knowledge should be used wisely and with sensitivity.

It may be that you have found something out or are just about to. Hidden truth is uncovered. But what now? You must consider the most constructive way to make use of this knowledge. The Hazel can provide nourishing nuts but also poisonous milk. Likewise newly found knowledge can be used creatively and constructively or critically and maliciously. So be warned, for as its says in the Book of Job: "They that plough iniquity, and sow wickedness, shall reap the same".

It may be that you find this newly gained knowledge challenging. The way that you allow this knowledge to affect you, your own optimism or pessimism, may be under question here. Is your cup half empty or half full? If you have found something out that you are finding hard to deal with then look for the silver lining in the cloud.

Hazel is a tree of high energy and you may be being drawn to it because you are suffering from a sense of stagnancy in your life. The Hazel suggests a variety of ways to build up your energy: travel, being near to running water, dancing, running. It may also be that you need to communicate and get something off your chest. It can be a surprise too see how much we can bottle up inside ourselves. A very effective way to move blocked feelings is to write them down. You will find, when you free yourself from carrying the burden of locked in feelings, that your energy levels increase wonderfully.

Heather

Latin name: *Erica vulgaris*
Ogham name: Ura

The Celts regarded Heather as a messenger from the spirit world. In wild, open moorlands one never feels quite alone. On their journeys across the heath Celtic travellers would have heard the spectral sounds of the wind across the Heather and would have imagined these as the voices of spirits from another realm. From a modern perspective Heather can also be seen as a symbol for messages that come from our subconscious. The barren landscape of moorland presents our eyes with a visual emptiness which our imagination can fill will images from our unconscious mind.

The Bach flower remedy is said to be 'generous, understanding and willing to help others'. Heather is certainly generous in its uses. After the forest clearances in Scotland the Heather that grew on the resulting moorland provided a wealth of materials, including roofing, fuel, ropes, beer, tea, dyes and even food for sheep. Heather honey has a sweet, flower like flavour and is a delicacy.

Heather has been used in traditional medicine for thousands of years. It is a mild sedative and has antiseptic properties. A bath of heather water can soothe the pains of rheumatism.

White Heather is a lucky charm. It was said to protect against acts of passion, a hint that Celtic society could be violent and brutal.

Red Heather is a symbol of passion. It was sacred to Aphrodite, Venus and other Goddesses of love. It was also sacred to Isis who found her brother/lover Osiris imprisoned in a Heather tree.

From Asia Minor spread the worship of the Queen Bee Goddess, a Goddess of all living things. The Heather was sacred to this Goddess and in summer the sight of bees busy above the Heather flowers would have evoked an image of faithful subjects serving their Queen. The Greeks and Romans inherited the worship of the Queen Bee Goddess and transferred Her qualities to Aphrodite and Venus.

The qualities of heather are: generosity, help, messages, luck and passion.

Divinatory message: Heather

Good luck is at hand. Whatever your question you can expect a good outcome.

It is possible that this outcome will depend upon help from other people. Consider now who would be willing and able to help you and be aware that in asking for their help you will be giving them a valuable gift.

We often have a great reluctance to ask for what we need. This may be connected to a fear of rejection, or a feeling that we have not got the right to ask for what we want. Try to put yourself in the place of the person who you would like to ask for help? Would you reject a call for help from one of your friends? Then why should they reject your call for help?

Insulated as we our in our modern lives we are losing the sense of community and mutual support which has been a vital lifeline for previous generations. Some neighbours can spend years without even speaking to each other. We should make the effort to maintain a connection with those around us, for they need us and we need them.

Heather indicates the need to be open to messages from your subconscious. These may come in dreams or in intuitive flashes, in strange coincidences or in gut feelings. We have been brought up to dismiss our intuitions, to defer to the authority of experts, facts and statistics. Yet you will find that your intuition is rarely wrong. Try to look inside yourself and see what your feelings are telling you. Perhaps you have an urge to contact someone, if so then go and make that telephone call. Maybe you are craving a certain type of food: trust your body to know what it needs. Respect your own feelings.

Heather is sacred to the Goddess Venus, the Goddess of passion. Society imposes much pressure on us to stay in control, to inhibit our passions. It is important to learn self control, but having learnt it we may then have to learn again the joyous abandonment of childhood. If you are feeling inhibited at present then the Heather is encouraging you to let yourself go. Dance wildly, make love passionately, enjoy a good meal, shout, jump, laugh, cry, play. The Goddess says:

> Let my worship be within the heart that rejoices,
> For all acts of love and pleasure are my rituals.

HOLLY

Holly

Latin name: Ilex aquifolium
Ogham name: Tinne, meaning fire.

The holly can grow into a small tree although it is usually encountered as a shrub. It is famous for its tough, prickly dark green leaves and the red berries. Holly has become an essential Christmas decoration. As an evergreen, Holly is a token of immortality and it has always been a symbol for the immortal Gods. It is appropriate that Jesus, inheriting the role of the reincarnated God from pagan traditions should also have inherited the Holly. In the carol 'The Holly and the Ivy' the Holly 'bears the crown' for this reason.

The Holly is a plant of good omen. It is a plant of protection against evil or angry spirits and wards off lightning.

The Holly King is one of the names of the pagan God Tannus, also known as the Wild Man, the Green Man and Jack in the Green. The Holly King rules the waning year, from the summer solstice to the winter solstice. At mid-winter the Oak King defeats the Holly King to rule over the waxing year. At the Summer solstice the Holly King wins back the crown. Memories of this struggle were preserved in Arthurian legend where Sir Gawain (summer) fights an annual battle with the Green Knight (winter), who was armed with a holly club.

The Bach flower remedy is used for any kind of strongly negative state such as anger, jealousy, bitterness, envy, rage, suspicion, revenge or hatred. All of these emotions can be seen in the eyes and in homeopathy Holly is used for eye

93

complaints. The eye is the organ associated with light. Likewise the Holly denotes light, heat and fire. Holly charcoal burns very hot and is ideal for forging steel. The shiny leaves are very reflective of light and for this reason Holly can be a remedy against the winter blues if a branch is placed in rooms where the pale winter light does not penetrate.

The Druids decorated their dwellings with Holly during winter believing that this would provide an abode for the sylvan spirits of the woods.

The Holly is sacred to the Gods of lightning, especially Thor. Its Celtic name, Tinne, has the same root as the Celtic thunder god - Tannus.

Magic using Holly is projective, that is to say it involves using your will to influence the world. For example throwing a Holly wand towards an animal was said to make the animal to obey the will of the thrower.

The qualities of Holly are good omens, protection against evil spirits and co-operation with good spirits. The Holly is both spiky and an evergreen and so magically combines the protective qualities of thorns with the regenerative qualities of evergreens.

Divinatory message: Holly

The Holly and The Oak represent the dual, complementary aspects of the Horned God of the Celts. Both Holly and Oak represent your relationship with the divine.

The Oak represents the radiant, outgoing God of the waxing sun. It counsels you to connect with divine will and follow the path of the mystic. In the Tarot this is the path of the High Priest, the Emperor and the Hermit.

The Holly represents the darker God of the waning year. His is the path of the magician and counsels you to connect with your divine power. In the Tarot this is the path of the Magician, the Fool and The Hanged man.

The truly great religious leaders have mastery over both paths. During the first thirty years of his life Jesus was a mystic, but during his ministry he became a man of action, turning the money lenders out of the temple, healing the sick and fighting hypocrisy and oppression. Gandhi and Martin Luther King provide other good examples of spiritual leaders who had a dramatic impact on the world.

In the Kabbalah, the inner and mystical teachings of Judaism, these two paths are clearly defined. The method of action involves translating spiritual ideas into physical reality. This could involve a whole range of things such as: delivering an inspiring speech, writing a book, performing a ritual, healing. The method of action corresponds to the path of the Holly. The method of devotion is seen in prayer, in meditation and in loving obedience. This is the path of the Oak.

So the message of the Holly is that the will of the divine wishes to work through you. You must put your ego aside and trust in the protective power of the divine. Connect to your divine self and find out what action is asked of you. This may portend a rebirth for you, an initiation into your higher self or a major change to your lifestyle.

When life challenges us to do the right thing we can sometimes be faced with a multitude of fears and doubts. There can also be pressure from the people around us to conform to what best suits them. The Holly is asking you to open your eyes. It is shining its light so that you can see the way ahead that is right for you.

Like a knight of old, you are on a spiritual quest. You may face ordeals and challenges but must strive to act from the will of your higher self. The protective qualities of the Holly serve as a reminder that those that follow a spiritual path are always protected by the Great Spirit.

Líme

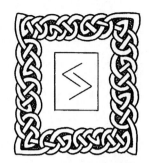

Latin name: *Tilea Europoea*

Lime (also known as Linden) is a graceful, tall tree with distinctive heart shaped leaves. The tree itself slightly resembles an upturned heart. The wood is light and fine grained, making delicate carvings. The wood is never eaten by worms. This fact has the practical advantage of making it useful in furniture making. It also gives a clue to the magical properties of the wood: it is ideal for warding off the forces of decay.

Lime flower tea is a relaxing remedy for nervous tension. It also soothes coughs and fevers. In homoeopathy, Lime is associated with the treatment of weakness of the eye and dimness of vision. It can also strengthen inner vision: ancient Scythian sorcerers used Lime to aid prophecy. The tree clears mists from both the physical eyes and the 'third eye'.

In Germany and Holland the Linden is often planted at the heart of the village. It is the tree of the Goddess Freyja, who together with the God Frey ruled the Vanir, the pantheon of the old Norse gods. Over the centuries these two deities have evolved into the Lord & Lady of Wicca, and so the Lime is the tree of the Goddess of the witches. Freyja and the Village Linden tree both symbolise the natural justice which rules over nature, love, feminine power and nature magic. Linden is the lovers tree where couples would go to receive the blessing of the Goddess. The tree's delicate leaves were thought to be like the Lady's hands and the lovers would feel Her blessed touch under the Linden.

The qualities of this tree are: Feminine Power, Natural Justice, Clear Seeing, the blessings of love and the soothing of the nerves. It is the tree of the heart.

Divinatory message: Lime

This tree brings the blessings of the Mother Goddess. It draws your attention to feminine power. If you are a woman, be aware of your own strengths. Perhaps you need to spend some time meditating upon the true strengths of womanhood. If a man, the message to you is to put aside your harsh male logic for a while. Connect to the truths that come from your animal nature (your anima), from your intuition and from the women around you.

This is the tree of clear seeing. There has been a fog before your eyes - you may have lost your way in it! Connect to the Goddess, to love and to your intuition and the fog will clear for you. The Lime is the tree of prophecy, so look inside yourself for a symbol or message to guide you on your way.

If your nerves have felt frayed lately and if you are suffering from the symptoms of stress then imagine yourself sat beneath the soft leaves of the Linden. Visualise the tree's love (the love of the Goddess) pouring into you from the touch of those cool leaves.

Love is one of the great feminine powers. Indeed the meaning of this tree can be seen in a mother's love for her child: her clarity of purpose, her nurturing, her strength. To be in love is a special form of clear seeing which gives an undeniable purpose to life. If you are in love the message of this tree for you is to believe in the truth of it and follow wherever it leads.

99

Oak

Latin name: *Quercus robur*
Ogham name: Duir

The Oak justly bears the title 'King of the Forest'. It is not only one of the most familiar of trees, but also one that has inspired much imagery, becoming part of our national consciousness. The Oak is a traditional symbol of England, at one time being engraved upon our silver coins. Indeed it seems a far more appropriate symbol than the lion, which in fact is an heraldic symbol of the English Monarchy first used in the time of Richard I, near the end of the twelfth century.

Oak wood is hard and tough and the tree has deep strong roots. The following saying emphasises the longevity of the tree:

> An Oak is three hundred years growing
> Three hundred years blowing
> And three hundred years decaying.

The Oak can grow to an enormous girth. The massive 'King Arthur's round table' in Winchester was made from a single slice of a great oak tree.

To the Druids the Oak was the most important tree. Indeed the name 'Druid' may mean 'Person of the Oak'. The Oak grove was the sacred cathedral of the Druids. Mistletoe found growing on English Oak (which it does rarely) was seen as a potent sign of divine blessing.

The Oak Bach flower remedy is prescribed for those strong, reliable people who shoulder great burdens without complaint. They are prone to taking on more than they can cope with and suffering breakdown. Herbally Oak is an astringent tonic. Carrying an acorn is said to preserve health and youth and gives luck and protection.

The rune ascribed to Oak is Ac. This encapsulates the power of the acorn in which continuous and mighty growth comes from small beginnings. It should be used to reinforce magic which assists the creative and productive process.

It is said that the roots of an oak spread as far below ground as its branches rise into the air. For this reason the tree symbolises the rule of divine will which holds sway in both the upper and the underworlds. This reflects the pagan concept of the underworld which was not seen as a place of hell beyond God's rule but rather as a part of the natural world still under divine influence. When Persephone was trapped in the underworld of Hades it was the sky god Zeus who commanded Hades to allow Persephone's return.

The Oak is associated with the sky Gods. To name a few: Taranis (Celtic), Thor (Scandinavian), Yayweh (Hebrew), Zeus (Greek), Jupiter (Roman) and Perkunas (Lithuanian). Given that they are sacred to the sky Gods, acorns and oak wood are considered to be a protection against being struck by lightning, even though the tree itself attracts lightning. A talisman can be made by taking two small oak twigs and tying them in the shape of an equal armed crossed with red cotton. Carried in the pocket this will not only be a defence against lightning but also give strength, balance and protection.

The British Horned God is also associated with the Oak. The spirit of Herne the Hunter was said to be found near an Oak tree in Windsor forest. This association can also be seen in the myths of the Oak King and the Holly King who rule over each half of the year.

The qualities of the Oak are: divine will, strength, endurance, protection and steady growth from small beginnings.

Divinatory message: Oak

There is a Hindu mantra called the Gayatri which sums up the message of the Oak well:

> Radiant sun, source of all energy
> who illuminates and sustains the world
> We open our hearts and minds to your light
> And become activated to do your will

The only true protection available in this volatile world is that obtained when we align our will with that of the great spirit. This is the only source of true strength. Therein lies the strength to build cathedrals and to move mountains. Therein lies the power to fight oppression and win liberation.

The power of the Oak is seen in the process of evolution. The wonders of the natural world have been built over many millions of years. Oak power is immense, but it is in no rush. Change will come about but may take many lifetimes.

The message of the Oak is that you must connect to the divine and then do its will. You may not see things change overnight, but you can be sure that each of your actions, each of your prayers will be part of the inexorable and unstoppable process of evolution to a better world.

The Oak asks us to consider our priorities. When seen from the greater scheme of things many of the issues that trouble us can seem petty. It is easy to get worked up about small things, to make mountains out of molehills. When this happens it is time to get some perspective. In your mind picture a great Oak that has lived for hundreds of years. How would he see the quibbles of your daily life? Stand back, decide what is really important to you and then give your attention to that.

The great root system of the Oak is a reminder that our inner growth is as important as material acquisitions. You may be at a stage in your life where external achievements are less of a priority to you and instead you have to work at developing yourself. Give yourself permission to indulge this need for inner under-standing. Your spiritual evolution is at stake here. Trust that your life has purpose and know that every challenge that you face is an opportunity to fulfil that purpose through inner growth.

Poplar

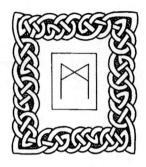

The Aspen and the White Poplar are the two native British Poplars but the Black Poplar has been resident here for hundreds of years. The tall slender upright Poplar, resembling a spire, which is commonly planted as a wind-break and alongside roads is the Lombardy Poplar. It was introduced into Britain in 1758 by Lord Rochford and originates from the Himalayas.

Black Poplar (*Populus nigra*)

The Black Poplar is a tree sacred to Hecate in her role as the death Goddess. It is a tree associated with burial practices and symbolises loss of hope. There is a countryside tradition of burying a docked lamb's tail under a Poplar tree at lamb-docking time, an offering to the Goddess to protect the lambs themselves.

The black resin that weeps from the tree's bark has been called 'amber tears'. This has been associated in legends with the bitter weeping of the sisters of Phaethon, son of Helios the Sun God. Phaethon stole his fathers chariot (the sun) and rode it so recklessly that it almost set fire the earth. Zeus was so angry that he killed Phaethon with a bolt of lightning. The weeping sisters of Phaethon, who had encouraged him to steal the chariot, were turned into Black Poplar trees and their tears became the amber balsam on their bark.

105

POPLAR

The qualities of this tree are loss of hope and tears of regret.

White Poplar (*Populus alba*)

In Homer's Odyssey White Polar was one of the three trees of resurrection (the others being Alder & Cypress). The White Poplar and Alder were sacred to Persephone, the Goddess of regeneration. This association with resurrection goes back thousand of years. In Mesopotamia around 3000 BC the dead were buried wearing head-dresses of White Poplar leaves to symbolise their resurrection.

In Greek mythology the valley surrounding the Styx, the river which was crossed at death, was full of White Poplar trees. This may have been to comfort the dead by reminding them of the certainty of their resurrection.

The qualities of Poplars are resurrection and regeneration.

Divinatory message: Poplar

Black and White Poplar represent Death and Rebirth. The leaves of the trees have a light and a dark side and the flashing of the moving leaves was said to convey the passage of time. The Poplar is therefore a potent symbol of the cycles of nature: day and night, summer and winter, the in breath and the out breath, expansion and contraction, birth and death.

The Poplar reminds us that life is constantly subject to change. As William Blake said, life is like sand in the palms our hands, if we try and grasp it too tightly it will just slip between our fingers.

It can often be hard to accept change. There is security and comfort in familiar things. However change will come for we cannot hold back the tide. In the natural world the most successful creatures have been the ones that have adapted to change. Likewise with us, the more adaptable we are the more we can get out of life.

Examine the changes that are taking place around you. What is new? What has gone? Ask yourself how you have adapted to take account of these changes. If you have stayed the same despite these changes then ask yourself why. Are you trying to deny that things have changed? Do you believe that things should have stayed the same? Can you turn back the clock?

If you have acknowledged the changes that have taken place around you then it is now time to look for the opportunities that this will bring. Don't let events pass you by. If we cry for too long for that which is lost, our tears will turn to amber. Remember the phoenix that rises out of its own ashes. This myth hints that the future holds the promise of treasures unimagined. Embrace change and live a life of constant resurrection.

Rose

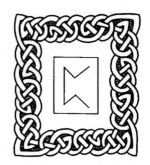

Latin name: *Rosa canina*

There is a wide variety of wild Roses, the most common being the Dog-Rose. This was so called because in medieval times it was believed that it was a cure for rabies and dog bites. Other indigenous Roses include the Field Rose, the Sweet Briar, the Burnet Rose and the Downy Rose.

Roses have been cultivated for thousands of years and it is likely that they were first bred in Persia. The cultivation of Roses later spread through Palestine to Greece and Rome. The Romans made luxurious use of Rose petals, often using them to carpet floors and even the streets. The Rose was sacred to Flora, the Goddess of flowers and Hymen, the God of marriage. The Romans even believed that wearing Rose garlands would prevent drunkenness.

The flower of the uncultivated Rose forms a natural pentagram, making it sacred to the earth Goddess. To the Romans the Rose was the flower of Venus and the badge of her priestesses. As a symbol of womanhood the Rose was transported into Christian iconography, becoming a symbol for Mary.

There was a medieval tradition of hanging a Rose above the dinner table to remind the diners that confidences must be kept secret. This has come down to us in the form of the plaster ceiling Rose and the expression 'Sub Rosa', meaning 'in secret'. The Rose-Cross is an important symbol for a number of secret and Masonic societies. It shows a Rose at the

110

centre of an equal armed cross and symbolises the incarnation of spirit within matter. Each arm of the cross represents one of the four elements of the material world, the Rose adds the fifth element of spirit which incarnates matter with life.

The Rose is a symbol both of womanhood and of secrecy, and appropriately it is also a symbol of a woman's genitalia.

Roses are said to be 'good for the skin and the soul'. The oil extracted from the petals are a staple of the beauty industry and a pungent and healing aromatherapy essence. Rose hips (from the dog Rose) have provided a vital source of vitamin C in times when fresh fruit and vegetables are unavailable. Anacreon summarised the medicinal virtues: 'the Rose distils a healing balm, the beating pulse of pain to calm'.

The qualities of the Rose are womanhood and secrecy.

Divinatory message: Rose

A man will be familiar with the association between womanhood and secrecy. A woman's body echoes the phases of the moon with her blood flow and bears life within her womb. These are holy mysteries. A woman knows the secret depths of her power and strength. In many cultures women make time for themselves to share their mysteries.

The message of the Rose is that these mysteries are calling you. For a man this may mean attraction and love for a woman or it may mean that it is time for him to explore the woman within himself, his anima. It may be worth asking yourself which of your needs you are expecting the woman in your life to fulfil. Is it now time for you to develop these qualities in yourself? Until a man has found the ability to mother himself, he will always expect his partner to do this for him. Is that a sound basis for an adult relationship?

For a woman the Rose is a sign that she needs to contact the deep secret powers within herself. These female powers are an invincible source of strength, the depth of which no man could even imagine. Make contact with other women, share and support each other. Take the time to appreciate yourself as a woman. The Rose encourages you to question your own inhibitions. Challenge the voices that hold you back, that say: "You can't do that because...". These voices do not speak the truth. They are the voices of patriarchal control and they lie.

The Rose hints at secrets. You may be in a place where you are having to keep something secret, or may feel that something is being hidden from you. If so, then do not get anxious about this. Trust that the truth will come out in its own way, when appropriate.

Rowan

Latin name: *Sorbus aucuparia*
Ogham name: Luis, meaning radiance

There is a lonely rowan tree clinging to the steep sides of a hill just above an icy stream high in the Pennines. This tree is near to a place called Snake Pass in the Dark Peak. This seems appropriate given that in legend snakes or dragons were said to guard the rowan tree. In winter the shiny silvery grey bark and determined knottiness of the tree bestow a noble magic upon the bleak hill. In summer the bright red berries are a spectacular contrast of colour against the grey stone and dull heather of the Dark Peak. This rowan tree is an altar of life in a rugged cathedral of nature.

The mythology of the rowan reflect the hardy nobility of its spirit. This spirit is also reflected in its many common names: mountain-ash, wild-ash, quicken, quickbeam, witchen, witchwood, witchbane, eye's delight. The tree has white flowers and red berries. White and red are the colours of the Goddess and so the tree marks itself out as a tree sacred to Her. Two qualities of the Goddess in particular are associated with the tree: protection and vision.

Protection: The berries of the rowan have a small pentagram on them. The pentagram is one of the primary pagan symbols of protection. In Norse mythology the Rowan saved Thor from being swept away by the otherworld river Vimar by reaching one of its branches into the water to him. Rowan amulets are used to provide protection from drowning. Incense from the leaves and berries can be used to banish unwanted energies.

113

The tree was often planted near to stone circles to protect the energy of these places.

At the beginning of May sheep were passed through a hoop made of rowan to guard their health. Likewise milk churns were circled with branches of the tree to protect them from evil. It is clear that in the days when diseases and bacteria were little understood the sudden illness of an animal or souring of milk could be seen as the cause of evil influences. The tree was seen as a powerful protection from such malevolence. Rowan was also regarded as a potent protection for people. At Hallowe'en an equal armed cross made by tying two rowan sticks with red ribbon was carried to ward off malignant spirits. In Scotland rowan twigs were hung over stables to protect the livestock.

Vision: Rowan twigs were used to make the rods used by dowsers to detect metal. These were sometimes called 'witches' wands'. The Druids used the smoke from rowan fires to invoke their spirit guides. The visionary power of the tree stems from its connection to the earth dragon, the subtle network of energy streams that course through the earth and often connect at sacred sites.

To the Druids poetry was not a sterile exercise in versification but was the bringing into words of visions from other realms of being. Their muse was the Goddess Brigit who was herself a poet. Brigit possessed three arrows made of rowan wood. These three arrows symbolise many things including the triple nature of the White Goddess as maiden, mother and crone and Brigit's three attributes: inspiration, healing and the protection of the hearth. They may also symbolise the 'third eye' that sees beyond the mundane world.

The qualities of the tree are the protection and vision that comes from connecting to the energies of the earth.

Divinatory message: Rowan

In its strong, serpentine roots the Rowan connects to the deep rivers of energy that snake through the earth, and through these it connects to the Earth Goddess whose nervous system is made up of these energy lines. To connect to this energy gives protection and vision.

If this tree is calling you then you now have a great need to connect to these powerful energies. This may be a critical time for you - like Thor you are being carried away by the river of your deepest motivations. To escape from the river you must reach out and make a connection to something that will anchor you back in life as firmly as the Rowan is anchored by its roots. This may mean making a connection to the divine, to a person, to a place; only you will know. For you do know that something or somebody is now reaching out to you. It is up to you to reach out and regain your roots. The tree was regarded by the Druids as the tree of life. Its message to you is to reconnect to the realities of life and to anchor yourself in them.

You may feel that you can no longer make sense of your life, you cannot see where you are going. Rowan wood was used to make spinning wheels. The spinning wheel is an ancient symbol of fate. To find the sense of purpose that you are looking for you may need to look beyond the tree to see the wood. The cloth of fate that the Goddess has woven for you will tell a meaningful story, but to see it you will have to stand back from the threads from which it is finely woven. Relax and visualise the Goddess before you weaving the tapestry that tells the story of you life. Look at how the threads of the tapestry are woven together to form pictures. On these pictures see the patterns of your life, the story that is unfolding. Connect to your sense of who you are and know that there is meaning in your life.

This would be a good time to turn your sense of meaning into poetry or art. Explore the enjoyment and therapy that can be obtained from expressing yourself in these ways. Your poetry or art does not have to be 'good' by any standard other than that it expresses your own truth. If it does that then it is priceless. Weave your creativity together with your inner vision and see how the two feed each other. Connect!

SCOTS PINE

Scots Pine

Latin name: *Pinus sylvestris*

The Scots Pine is Britain's only true native Pine tree. When grown tall its greenery seems to float like clouds high up the trunk. The bark has a lovely colour, ranging from coppery brown to orange. The leaves have a blue tint and when seen from a distance the trees appear to be surrounded by a blue haze. The sweet scent of the tree is both aromatic and cleansing - the essential oil is a powerful disinfectant.

The Pine has associations with birth, new life and fresh energy. Storks, the harbingers of new life, build their nests in Pine trees. In the Orkneys new-born babies and their mothers were purified by having a blazing Pine torch whirled three times around their bed. The Pine tree was sacred to Osyris, the Egyptian God of new life. The cones are used as a phallic symbol and carrying a Pine cone is said to increase fertility. This custom derives from the worship of Bacchus, the God of fecundity. Priests of Bacchus carried the thyrsus, a wand tipped with a Pine cone to evoke his rampant sexuality.

The tree gives off a strongly charged positive energy. This is the tree of illumination. The rune Ken (also called Kano) ties these associations together. It is the rune of Pine trees, morning light, bonfires and openings - especially openings that let in new light. A Pine branch can be used as a bright torch.

The resin that seeps from Pine bark creates a very purifying incense. It can be burnt to clear a space of negative energy

119

and let the light back in. The scent of Pine is especially beneficial to people who suffer from the winter blues.

At midwinter the Druids held dramatic fire festivals, burning the oily wood of Pine on massive bonfires and hanging lights and reflective objects in Pine trees. These festivals were held to halt the retreat of the sun and to herald the new year. From these fire festivals we have inherited Christmas trees and the custom of burning the Yule Log.

Pine is used within the Bach flower remedies to dispel darkness. It is used to dispel self-reproach, guilt and self blame. The essential oil has the same benefits in aromatherapy.

The qualities of the tree are fertility, new light and new life.

Divinatory message: Pine

This tree signifies illumination and new life in all senses of these words.

It is no longer appropriate to dwell on the past and criticise yourself for past mistakes. There is a great opportunity for renewal in your life right now. This may be an opportunity for new growth or may be a new perspective throwing new light on things for you. You must connect with the positive energy that is around you. Make room to let new light in.

New projects will go well at present. If you have been putting something off for a while then now is the time to get it started. You should find that you have abundant energy for anything that is new.

After a dark night the light of a new day can have a remarkably restorative effect. In winter we can become starved of daylight, especially if our working conditions keep us indoors during the daylight hours. Ensure that you feed yourself some sunlight every day: go for a walk at lunchtime and get out at the weekends. Other arboreal remedies for the winter blues include burning pine essential oil and hanging holly branches in the dark corners of your rooms.

You may have reached a time when feelings of guilt about something that happened in the past are no longer appropriate. Transform this guilt into positive action and move on.

The strong associations of the Pine with fertility may indicate that conception or childbirth are possibilities at the moment. You have been warned!

SILVER FIR

Silver Fir

Latin name: *Abies alba*
Ogham name: Ailim

The Silver Fir is the tallest native European tree and can grow up to 220 feet tall. Fir cones can be used to predict rain: they close up when it rains and open out in sunlight.

The Fir shares much of the mythology of the Pine, both being associated with childbirth. The Fir is however much more of a female tree, being associated with Goddesses such as Artemis, the Goddess of childbirth and Athena, the city protectress. The Trojan horse was said to have been made from the wood of the Silver Fir in honour of Athena, the protectress of Troy. The Pine is more closely related to Gods such as Bacchus, God of fecundity. A further distinction would be to say that the Fir is the tree of birth, whereas the Pine is the tree of conception.

Throughout European mythology a common theme persists. The divine child that is born of the Goddess under the Silver Fir is the God Himself, who both was and will be the lover of the Goddess and so hence his own father. This self-procreation of the God is seen in the seemingly incestuous story of Osyris and Isis. It is also embodied in the story of Jesus who was both the son of God and is one with God.

These stories originate in the early Mediterranean mystery cults and represent the cycles of nature. The corn that is cut at the end of the old year become the seeds from which the corn of the new year grows. The Silver Fir is a symbol of this

123

regenerative aspect of nature because when cut down and seemingly dead, new stems will appear from the roots.

In 'The White Goddess' Robert Graves contrasts the Silver Fir with the Yew. They are both evergreens. However whereas the Yew symbolises death the Fir symbolises birth and new life. Graves wrote:

Fir, womb of silver pain
Yew, tomb of leaden grief,
Viragoes of one vein,
Alike in leaf-
With arms up flung
Taunt us in the same tongue:
'Here Jove's own coffin-cradle swung'

In fact Graves is botanically mistaken as the leaves of the Silver Fir and Yew are easily distinguished. Yew leaves have wide dark green needles growing regularly along the twigs in two distinct flattened rows. Silver fir needles are smaller, silvery on the underside and branch out in a graceful spiral around the twig.

The qualities of the tree are birth, beginnings and regeneration.

Divinatory Meaning: Silver Fir

This tree is an indicator that a birth or a new beginning is at hand. All beginnings present the opportunity for things to be better. However it is vital to avoid complacency for old habits can soon slip back. If you have selected this tree then it would be a good idea to consider what your 'new year resolutions' would be. The time is right to make some fresh commitments.

The Silver Fir is the tree of regeneration and recycling. Take a look at what you have and see what new uses you can put this material to. This applies on various levels. It may mean putting some physical object to a new use or may mean reviewing your talents and seeing how these can be used in a different way. We have many transferable skills but sometimes fail to realise how useful they can be.

The tree challenges us to be more thoughtful about recycling. Nature re-uses everything that dies. Yet we are immensely wasteful as a species. If everyone put a little effort into sorting their rubbish then we would have a vast resource available to us. The Fir also challenges us to re-evaluate our need for 'new' things. The advertising industry puts immense pressure on people to buy new cars, new clothes and so on. Yet much that can be bought second hand is of very high quality. The planet cannot sustain the wasteful consumption that we have in the west and which we are now exporting to developing countries.

If you can reframe your definition of the word 'new' then you can begin to really appreciate all the things you have. Everything we have can be seen anew. Even people that we think familiar can be seen in a new light. Try this experiment: imagine that everything is completely new to you, open your eyes to the things around you. How much do you notice that you never saw before? Complacency and familiarity are a form of blindness. Open your eyes!

Spruce

Latin name: *Picea abies*

The Norway Spruce is the tree most commonly used for Christmas trees. It is an upright conifer that can grow up to 50 metres tall. The tree is shallow rooted and does not have a taproot, making it vulnerable to being blown over in strong winds. It takes around 10 years for the Norway spruce to grow to six feet, at which time the trees can be harvested for Christmas. As the Yule tree it is the symbol of eternal life.

To the Vikings, the tall pole of the tree's trunk was regarded as a symbol of the world's axis. It was a reminder that despite the changes and instabilities of human life there is permanence in the natural world. The concept of a pole at the centre of the earth was common to both Nordic and native American views of the world. The Sioux used a pole made from the straight trunk of the Cottonwood tree as the centrepiece of their ceremonies. This pole represented the link between the earth and the sky and the covenant between the people and the Great Spirit.

Over the last two decades Norway spruce has been subject to die-back caused by air pollution and acid rain. This has had a drastic effect on the great forests of northern Europe, where the Spruce is the most important tree. This tragedy serves as a clear and unequivocal warning to us that we must stop polluting our environment.

Resonant spruce wood is used for sounding boards in pianos and the bodies of violins, as well as for boats and barrels. It is used in the manufacture of pulp and paper. The new, leafy shoots are used to brew spruce beer.

The qualities of the tree are permanence and eternal life.

Divinatory Message: Spruce

The Yule tree is a reminder that there is a natural order to the world and within that natural order an eternal promise of renewal. The earth turns, the seasons change and life follows an eternal cycle of birth, life, death and renewal. Nothing is wasted in this cycle. Energy is always conserved.

It may suggest that you are out of step with the natural order of things, possibly trying to fight against the inevitable cycle of change instead of going with the flow of it. However fearful you may be of change you can be certain of two things: change will happen and life will go on.

To those facing the suffering or expectation of bereavement this can seem a hard lesson. Yet death can be seen as the other side of life and it has been said that 'death is the birth of the soul'. Death has been a fact of life since the beginning of time for energy is always conserved. New life cannot come about unless old life gives back its energy to Gaia.

On a more global scale the Spruce serves as a reminder that those civilisations who try to deny the natural order and try to conquer nature always face the inevitable: the energy that they have taken out of the system will be taken back by the system. Gaia is a tolerant earth mother but we must not forget that she is the Goddess of all creatures. Human beings do not own Her. There is also the reminder that the pollutants that we produce as by products of our consumer lifestyles are going directly into the natural systems that support us.

128

The spruce may be telling you that it is time to review your life. What is really important to you? What things do you want to make permanent? It is important that you become clear about your priorities. The only way to ensure that something is permanent is to make a commitment to giving it your attention and your energy. You may also realise that you have been making a lot of effort to keep something or to prevent a change when in fact you are quite happy to let that thing go. You have been holding on from force of habit or from insecurity. Make a conscious choice to let go of the things that you no longer require and allow you energy to go to where it is really needed.

Sycamore

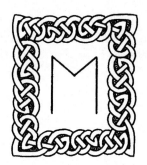

Latin name: *Acer pseudoplatanus*

The Sycamore is not a native British tree, but it has been grown here for the last five centuries and is now very common and familiar. It is notable for its heavy branched crown and winged fruits. The sycamore is a maple and is also known as the 'Great Maple'. Its leaves have the characteristic shape of maple leaves as seen in the flag of Canada. In Scotland the tree is often called the 'Plane' tree.

The trunk of the Sycamore yields a sweet saccharine juice. In the Scottish highlands this was used to make a palatable wine.

The tree is very hardy and grows quickly. This has ensured that it has naturalised itself very successfully. The tree will grow straight and tall even when exposed to bitter winds and sea breezes. It can grow to a height of 50 foot in as many years.

Sycamore has established itself as one of our favourite trees, enriching town and countryside alike. It seems a fitting symbol for the many waves of immigration that have taken place over the last two thousand years, constantly enriching our society. It is a symbol for how the very essence of our culture has constantly re-defined itself in terms of these new influences, taking on the best traditions of each.

The tree has always been valued, but perhaps its greatest admirer was Xerxes, The King of Persia (519-465 B.C.). He was said to have found a Sycamore so beautiful that he lavished it with gifts of jewellery and assigned a bodyguard to it.

Sycamore wood is soft and light, yet strong. It is used for cup and bowl turning and is used by saddle makers.

The qualities of the tree are integration and adaptation.

Divinatory message: Sycamore

On a personal level the message of this tree is that you should consider how best to assimilate and benefit from any new influences around you. Change and new things can cause anxiety but they also provide a wealth of opportunity. It is perhaps natural that we view anything new with suspicion. Some people will try to avoid the new, building up their fears in their own imagination. It may also be the case that the older we get, the less able we are to deal with the new. However when we make the effort to get to know the new then we are usually very pleasantly surprised for everything and everybody has something to offer.

There is also an encouragement to take pleasure from the simple things in life. They say that the best things in life are free! There is tremendous social pressure to indulge in expensive tastes. The advertisers are constantly pushing new products at us. With this drive to consume we can easily forget the value of things that cost us little such as the clear taste of a glass of tap water and the energising effects of a brisk walk in the fresh air. Think about the things that you consume and become aware of the forces that pressurise you into this consumption. Try to rediscover the simple things in life - the best things in life are free!

Willow

Latin name: *Salix alba*
Ogham name: Saille

Willows are usually found near water. White willow is a tall, straggly tree that can grow up to 60 feet tall. It has striking, dense silvery grey foliage. Willow is a very flowing tree. When growing beside a river the supple branches bend down into the water like a maiden trailing her hair in the flow. When the wind blows, the tree's foliage moves like wind blowing across the surface of water. When in full leaf the tree itself is like a cascade of water, each of its leaves reflecting the light like water dripping from the edge of a waterfall.

Willow roots follow water courses. They have the strength to wrap themselves around water pipes and break the pipe. The roots then follow the water up the pipes and have even been known to emerge out of bathroom sinks in their voracious search for water.

In the '*Lord of the Rings*' Tolkein portrays this creeping, clasping characteristic of the tree. Old Man Willow lulled the Hobbits to sleep under his cool branches and then drew them into his trunk before Tom Bombadill came to their rescue. Tolkein describes the willow vividly: "His great thirsty spirit drew power out of the earth and spread like fine root-threads in the ground".

A number of weeping willows are related to the white willow. The true weeping willow is from China and is rare in this country, usually being found in ornamental gardens. Willow

133

WILLOW

wood is good for basket making and fencing, being very supple. Cricket bats are made from a variety of willow grown specifically for the springy qualities of the wood.

The willow was sacred to various Goddesses including Hecate, Circe, Hera and Persephone. These goddesses are all associated with the moon, the underworld and wisdom. Hecate was a moon Goddess who was reputed to have taught witchcraft to humans. It was said that dogs howling at the moon were a sign of her approach. The Tarot card 'The Moon' shows two dogs beside water howling at the moon. This card captures all of these associations with the willow. It represents both illusion and the journey into the sub-conscious.

To the ancients the Dark Goddess of the moon was a powerful and ghastly figure. They knew instinctively the terrors of the dark side of human nature and projected these upon the death aspect goddesses. However these goddess were also revered as the source of wisdom. Athena clearly exhibits this dichotomy: she is the Goddess of Wisdom who provides help and succour to mankind and also the terrible Goddess of War who bears the aegis: a symbol of death made from the head of Medusa.

The popular image of the witch is similarly divided. On the one hand they were seen as wicked woman who had the evil eye. On the other hand they were respected as the wise women of the country who could provide healing and counsel. In the White Goddess Robert Graves states that the words 'witch', 'wicker' and 'willow' all derive from the same root. That root was probably the word 'wicce', meaning wisdom.

Witch's brooms were bound with willow, linking them to the witch's Goddess Hecate, and to the Moon. The broom's handle was made of Ash and its brush made of birch twigs. This was a symbol of fertility: the male Ash shaft being thrust into the female birch bush. Magically the willow is useful in spells for enclosing and turning back psychic attack.

Culpepper's *Herbal* confirms the lunar associations of Willow. He writes that 'the Moon owns it'. The tree's bark has been used to ease rheumatism. It contains Salicylic acid. This is a natural pain-killer from which aspirin was synthesised. The Bach flower remedy is used for those people who suffer any small adversity with bitterness and resentment. They are sulky, blame other people and feel hard done by. On a mental level the tree has the ability to cleanse the spirits.

The qualities of the tree are moon magic, enchantment, healing and the exploration of the subconscious.

Divinatory message: Willow

The discovery of the subconscious has meant that the projection of the darkest aspects of human nature upon the Moon Goddess is better understood. The integration of our shadow side is seen as the pathway to psychological health. In these terms the dichotomy in the image of the moon goddess can be resolved. The willow, the moon and the waters with which they are associated are all symbols of the personal and collective unconscious. This is not only the source of our dreams and motivations but also of our deepest wisdom.

The willow is the tree of the moon goddess and of the moon reflecting waters of the subconscious. This is a sign that you must now tap into the deep wisdom of your soul. It is time to become aware of how your motivations are directed by the tides of your subconscious. It is also time to tap into the richness of the collective unconscious.

This is not as hard as it may sound. You need to find a situation in which you can safely talk about yourself. A good friend may be willing to listen, but make it clear that you are not expecting them to 'solve' your problems for you - this would be a distraction. Alternatively there are now many counsellors available who are well trained in allowing their clients to find their own truth. When you have found an appropriate listener then set both time and space aside for yourself. Ask your listener if they can stay with you for an hour. Make sure that you will be free from interruptions.

Begin to talk about yourself. Give an overview of the place where you are at in your life. You could try some free association: say what comes into your head. If you remember a recent dream then you could relate that dream and try to unravel its meaning for you by exploring the symbols in the dreams and what relevance they have for you.

After a while some themes will emerge. If these bring up strong emotions then be reassured that you are starting to face up to things that can no longer be suppressed. Ask yourself how long these themes have been issues for you. You may well find that they go back a long way. Try to realise how deeply embedded in your subconscious these themes have become.

Try to see how many of the choices you make are in fact controlled by these hidden themes. Guided meditations can be bought on tape and these can be very effective in allowing you to explore hidden aspects of yourself.

For you this will be the beginning of a journey of discovery: of discovering who you really are. To make this journey you will need nothing sophisticated, just the opportunity to talk and to be heard, the time to write and to meditate.

The Willow is the tree of moonlight and of dreams. When you make the effort to get to know yourself your dreams will co-operate with you and will furnish you with many symbols, images and memories. Your dreams will also allow you to connect to the collective unconscious: the vast reservoir of ancestral wisdom. Like the voracious roots of the Willow, you will find that your knowledge of your inner self will grow with an unstoppable thirst for understanding.

Yew

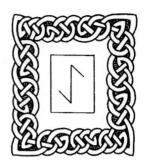

Latin name: *Taxus baccata*
Ogham name: Ioho

The Yew is an evergreen and can live for thousands of years. This longevity is possible because the tree regenerates its trunk from branches which root in the ground. In this way the tree will continue to increase its girth as it outlives civilisations.

The seeds and leaves of the tree are a deadly poison and it is said that on a hot summer's day the air around the tree is so thick with the tree's essence that it induces a death like sleep. Yew has another deadly characteristic. It is the wood that the English longbow was made from.

Taken together these characteristics make the tree a potent symbol of death, resurrection and immortality. For this reason the druids built their temples near Yew trees. When the sites of these temples were converted into churches the churchyards inherited the old yews. The symbolism was also carried into Christianity, the Yew becoming a symbol for the resurrection of Christ. Yew foliage is displayed in churches at Easter.

Yew is very toxic. The word 'toxin' itself is derived from the same root as the tree's Latin name: 'Taxus'. This toxicity relates the tree to lead and in turn to the planet of that metal, Saturn. In astrology Saturn rules time and old age and represents the inevitability of change. These could also be regarded as properties of the Yew.

At Samhain, the Celtic New Year, yew sprigs were handed out by the Druids to remind people to connect with the spirits of the departed and to appreciate the gift of life.

In Norse tradition the tree was sacred to the God Ullr, God of archery and winter. He lived in a sacred Yew grove called Ydair. The rune Eoh (also called Eihwaz) represents the Yew tree and defence. This rune can be used to dispel bad storms, in both the physical and emotional worlds. It signifies that change and movement will come, but without bad effect in the long term. It advises that it is best to live in the moment and to avoid wasting time waiting for tomorrow.

The Irish romance of Naoise and Deirdre illustrates the Yew's properties of death and immortality. The lovers' corpses were driven through with Yew stakes to keep them apart even in death. However each stake grew into a tree and these trees grew to embrace each other over the top of Armagh cathedral.

It seemed appropriate that the Alder, the tree of foundations, should be the first tree of this book. The Yew is equally appropriate as the final tree for it is the tree of endings. In the Celtic tree calendar the Yew was placed on the last day of the year, before the winter solstice. It also was the final vowel in the Celtic tree alphabet.

The qualities of the tree are eternity, death, re-birth and time-lessness.

Divinatory meaning: Yew

Yew trees are old beyond our comprehension. They have seen many civilisations pass. The oldest of them even pre-date history itself. With this long term perspective the concerns of a generation will seem trivial and the daily worries of a human being less than nothing.

The lesson of this tree is therefore to see things with a much longer perspective. The worries that you are cluttering your mind with today are trivial in the context of this lifetime, let alone the journey of your soul through the eternity of death and rebirth. Have faith that the pattern of your life will show stability in the long term and live for today.

The Yew is a reminder of death, but this reminder is not there to scare you but to encourage you to live the life you have.

In this life we are not immortal, but we spend much of our lives hiding from our mortality. We allow the days, months and years to drift by and forget that they can never be recaptured. A day will come that will be our last day. How many unfulfilled dreams will we take to that day? How many memories of days full of life, love and passion will we take there? The choice is ours and it is now.

The Wild Wood

(This chapter was written in collaboration with Mark Whittaker)

The sap which courses through each tree carries within it the most distant memories of humanity. When our ancestors lived as animals they knew how to listen. At the edge of survival, all living things spoke with a unique voice which was heard deep within the heart. Then we evolved and gained an awareness of our own identity. We were once a part of nature, but now we stand apart from it. We learnt to listen with our head and gradually our hearts became deaf. We learnt to give everything a label and forgot how to see. In time the natural world, once our home, became a place to be feared, controlled, destroyed.

Yet somewhere deep inside ourselves, deep in the primitive core of our organism, there lies a longing to hear again the voices of nature in our hearts. We seek a place of magic and mystery where life is lived on the edge. That place lies in our distant past, when we shared the earth with the trees.

The trees have not forgotten, they were old when we were young. For these reasons when we open our hearts to a big tree we hear voices unheard for millennia, for the sap which courses through the tree carries our most distant memories.

Our earliest ancestors lived in a state of intimate familiarity with all of the trees. Each tree would have been completely understood not only on a practical level but also as a personality. As the largest living things, trees would have been

143

given much respect, and people would realize that they had much to learn from them.

The early hunter gatherers who walked across Europe into what is now Britain would have found a land dense with warm forests. However in time the climate became colder and survival much harder. From these times small bands grouped together to create clearings in the forest which could be barricaded against animals and other hunting parties.

From this time onwards we started to feel safer hidden from nature than we did living within it. The vast forests surrounding the clearings would only be entered on necessity, to hunt for food or to trade. Within the clearings life became ordered, controlled and relatively secure.

Over time people's familiarity with the personalities of the forest became replaced by fears of the spirits and elves that were hidden within the wildwood.

When the Celts reached Britain the population expanded and the process of stockading continued. These stockades were not there as a protection against other humans - the Chieftain's hill fort served that purpose - but to hold back the wild animals of the forest and to keep in the domesticated animals. Gradually these stockades developed into well populated communities and eventually into towns.

More of the wildwood was cut back as agriculture developed. As the early farmers tried to maximize the productivity of the soil, suffering mystifying fluctuations in yield, they would have looked at the plethora of life in the wildwood with both awe and fear. Spirits of fecundity, obviously present in the forest, were entreated to increase the crops in the fields. Fertility rituals abounded which used the principals of sympathetic magic. Rituals were held in which the centre pieces were poles and staves freshly brought from the forest. Often individuals would be dressed entirely in foliage and leaves, as though one of the trees themselves had uprooted and walked into the village.

The Gods of these people reflected their awe of the wildwood. Cernunnos, the horned God of the forest was seen as being as dangerous and unpredictable as the elements of nature and he was treated with wary respect. In another guise he was worshipped as Herne the Hunter, the green masked God of the woods and consort of the Triple Goddess. This worship of the forest Gods has survived into this century in many folk tales. The legends of Robin Hood and Marion is a retelling of the marriage of the wild Herne to the virgin Goddess of the Land, a sacred mystery play which would have been repeated by country folk at fertility rituals held in the spring. When the Christian priests forbade the tales of the old Gods, the Gods were simply recast as folk heroes. Robin is Herne, the carefree young stag, courting danger and challenging the established ways. He is of the forest, a green man clad in its raiment. Marion is barely spoken of without her title of 'Maid' for she is the Triple Goddess in her maiden form, the Goddess of the fertile land.

Gradually the wild wood was conquered. The woods and forests came under the control of forester kings such as Richard I. When the Domesday book was compiled only a sixth of the wildwood stood intact. From that time on people began to take a far more utilitarian view of trees. Much of Britain's woodland was cut down to create wood for houses, ships and charcoal for fuel. In the villages and towns there were still a few people who retained knowledge of the herbal and magical properties of the trees. Yet in time even these wise men and women were seen as a threat to the developing professions of religion and medicine. The witch persecutions of the middle ages cut away our last links with the spirits of the wildwood.

Yet like a felled tree that sends up shoots from its splintered stump, the people of this land are again making a connection with the spirits of the forest. The anti-roads protesters who live in trees for months to prevent their destruction are bringing the voices of nature back to us. The vast expansion of interest in herbalism and tree-lore has begun to reveal the true value of the plants and trees around us. The new age interest in pagan religion and the rediscovery of the old Goddesses and Gods has given us back a nature based religion which puts us at ease with our own bodies and with the raw power of the natural world. The wisdom of our ancestors is perhaps nearer the surface of our unconscious minds than we may think.

Now the spirits of nature are making themselves felt again. At spiritual centres such as Findhorn people are working with the plant 'devas', the elemental life forms which inhabit plants and protect their growth. The equivalent spiritual entities which inhabit the tree world are the dryads. A dryad may be seen in anthropomorphic form such as a wood elf or it may be seen as strange lights around the tree. What is in fact happening is that the unconscious mind, which is in touch with the essential spirit of the tree, constructs a thought form to clothe the tree's energy. In this way the conscious mind is able to see an embodiment of the life-energy of the tree.

As more and more people develop the ability to communicate with devas and dryads we will find that nature is able to talk back to us and express its desperate need that the wildernesses are preserved in those few oases of wildwood that we have left.

Identifying the Trees

In order to help you gather a fallen twig from each of the 24 trees described in this book this section contains a brief description of the most characteristic features of each tree. To confirm these identifications, and to help you identify trees not covered here, I would recommend that you buy a good tree identification book such as the Larousse *'Easy Way Guide to Trees'*.

Alder

Alder is to be found alongside rivers. The bark of the alder is dark and looks rather scaly. The leaves are very round and do not come to a point. A key feature of the tree are what look like small dark brown, almost black, cones. These are in fact the female catkins and can be seen on the tree all year round.

Apple

The parent species to the cultivated apple is the Crab Apple. The blossom of the Crab Apple is white on top and pink underneath. The leaves of the tree have many small teeth running along the edge. The twigs often have short thorns.

Ash

The Common Ash marks itself out clearly by virtue of the large black buds to be seen along and at the tip of its branches. From autumn onwards there hang bunches of Ash 'keys' which ripen to a honey brown colour.

Aspen

The Aspen has a tall pole like trunk with a dark ridged bark. Its leaves are circular with gently wavy edges. The leaves have flat stalks which are the same length as the leaf itself. This causes the leaves to rustle in the breeze creating a whispering sound. The tree is most likely to be found in damp places. Its leaves are slow to rot, and its yellow leaves will lie fallen around the tree throughout the winter.

Beech

The Common Beech can grow into a wonderfully stately tree up to 40 metres tall. When growing in the open its girth can be nearly double its height. The bark of Beech resembles the grey sheen of elephant skin. Look out for the profusion of spiky nut casings around the base of the tree.

Birch

Silver Birch is a very distinctive tree. It has a tall graceful trunk. The higher branches angle upwards sharply but the lower branches are lateral. The tree has silver white bark which peels away in rings around its slender trunk. The trunks of older Birch trees often have whiskery ball like bumps on them.

Blackthorn

The best time to identify the Blackthorn is early spring (March or April) for it is one of the first trees to blossom. At this time it will display a mass of tiny white flowers which stand out strikingly against the dark wood of the tree. Blackthorn is usually grown in hedges and a look at its long, viciously sharp thorns will tell you why.

Elder

Elder has a soft corky appearance. Its wood is light and brittle. Examine the pith in any broken twigs. It will be very soft and spongy. In summer the tree flowers in clusters of creamy, sweet smelling flowers. In autumn these turn into a mass of berries, red at first becoming black when ripe.

Elm

To identify this tree in spring, look out for the transparent, flat, round seed casings. The seeds are held in a spot in the centre of the casing giving them an amoeba like appearance. The leaves are round and very green. At its base, the leaf extends further on one side of the stalk than the other, giving the impression that a small piece of leaf has been torn off from one side. The upperside of the leaf is hairy and feels like sandpaper.

Hawthorn

The Hawthorn is a dark, dense and thorny bush or small tree. Its leaves are very distinct. They are not too dissimilar in shape to small Oak leaves, but much more deeply lobed. From late May into June the tree will be awash with a mass of small white flowers. From September the red berries of the tree become ripe.

Hazel

The Hazel often has a shrub like appearance with many stems rising out of the ground like straight wands. The bark is shiny and it has many lateral lines running across its trunk. In early spring the tree is hung with long, droopy catkins which have a yellow-orange colour.

Heather

Heather is a small shrub which has suprisingly tough wood. It is commonly found on moorland and is easily identifiable when in flower.

Holly

Prickly, shiny green leaves. Red berries. It really needs no introduction!

Lime

The Common Lime is distinguished by the mass of lateral branches that spread up at its base. The broad, soft, succulent leaves of this tree have very delicate, small even teeth along their edge. The tree is often planted on streets and the cars beneath them become coated with the sticky sap which falls from the tree when aphids puncture the veins in the leaves.

Oak

We all know what acorns and Oak leaves look like. However the tree can grow into a surprising variety of shapes and sizes. The tree has an ancient, twisted, gnarled feel to it, especially when it grows in harsh conditions. Oaks have heavily forked branches because the leading shoots of the branches die easily and side shoots fork off in different directions.

Poplar

The White Poplar has maple like leaves with 3 to 5 lobes and white undersides. The tree can grow up to 35 metres tall but will remain slender with a heavily branching crown.

Rose

The Dog-Rose is a common plant which can often be found in hedgerows. Its flowers are delicately scented and palely pink. In autumn the bright red berry-like hips can be seen. When constructing your tree staves I would strongly suggest that you use the wood from a cultivated rose that has been pruned because you are less likely to find a fallen twig from a wild rose.

Rowan

From autumn and through the winter the Rowan is easily identified by its tight bunches of scarlet berries. The leaves of the tree are also quite distinctive. Matching pairs of finely toothed, thin oval leaves run down the side of each twig with a single leaf growing from the end of the twig. The bark of the Rowan resembles that of the Hazel, with what appear to be horizontal cut marks running around the trunk.

Scots Pine

To identify Pine look out for the stiff, pointy needles which grow from the branches in pairs. The leaves seem to hang in the crown of the tree like clouds.

Silver Fir

The needles of the Silver Fir are distinctive in that they spiral up the twigs in all directions. The cones rise vertically from the uppermost branches. The bark is smooth and grey on younger trees but becomes brown and cracked with age.

Spruce

Christmas Trees! The dark green needles grow from what look like small brown pegs. The cones droop down, whereas on Fir trees the cones stand erect on the stem. Spruce cones fall from the tree after the seeds have dispersed but Fir cones disintegrate on the stem.

Sycamore

The large, maple shaped leaves are quite distinctive and are usually covered with large black blotches and spots. The bark of the tree is grey-green with paler patches and also looks rather unhealthy. The twigs are almost always covered in a damp lichen.

Willow

The willow is usually found near water. Its leaves are long and thin with fine teeth and a furry underside. From the branches hang straight twigs which in winter are covered in small buds that look like claws.

Yew

Most old graveyards have a Yew or two. The tree has dark green, flat needles and a flaky red-brown bark. In old Yews the trunk can be very broad. From October the pinkish-red, cup shaped berries can be seen. Caution is required when collecting Yew as all parts of it are toxic.

Table of Correspondences

Tree(Ogham)	Summary of Meaning	Deities	Tarot card	Runes
Alder (Fearn)	Expressive and Oracular powers. Foundations.	Bran the blessed Cronos Saturn	Emperor	Uruz
Apple (Quert)	Sexual love, Health cleansing. The underworld.	Cerridwen Aphrodite, Venus Diana	Strength	Gebo
Ash (Nuin)	Travel, Journeys of the mind. The number 3. Rebirth.	Odin, Sky Gods	Chariot	Raido Ansuz
Aspen (Eoda)	A Shield that prevents fear. The quiet inner voice.	The Holy Spirit Guardian Angels	Fool	Isa
Beech (Phogos)	Sensitivity to wisdom, literature and beauty.	Jupiter Finn	Hanged One	Calc
Birch (Beith)	New Growth, purification, spring cleaning.	The Bright Maiden Bride/Bridget	Lovers	Berkana Ingwaz
Blackthorn (Straif)	Protective and projective magic. Psychic protection.	Kali The crone aspect of Triple Goddess	Tower	Algiz
Elder (Ruis)	magic, healing, divination. Crone Goddess.	The Dark Maiden The Elder-Mother The Cailleach	Temperance (1)	Erda
Elm (Lemh)	Purification, death, power of small, bad habits.	Gaia Mother Earth	Hermit	Ear
Hawthorn (Huathe)	Marriage, fertility, nourishment, protection	The Triple Goddess Olwen Cardea	Empress	Thurisaz
Hazel (Coll)	Wisdom and inspiration gained from connection to channels of energy	Mercury Thoth	Sun	Teiwaz
Heather (Ura)	Good luck. Aid.	Graine	Ace of Pentacles	Wunjo Sowelu
Holly (Tinne)	Protective magic. Dark God of waning year	The Holly King The Green Knight Mars Tammuz	Magician	Hagalaz

Tree	Meaning	Frigga / Justice	Justice	Jera
Lime	Feminine power. Natural justice. The blessings of love	Frigga Justice	Justice	Jera
Oak (Duir)	Light god of waxing year. Divine will. Strength Protection	The Oak King Sir Gawain Jove, Zeus, Thor	High Priest	Ac
Poplar	Resurrection. Regeneration. Polarities of black/white;Day/night	Persephone (White) Hecate (Black)	Judgement	Mannaz
Rose	Secrets, mysetries of womanhood. The anima	Isis Venus Mary	High Priestess	Perth
Rowan (Luis)	Connection with Earth energies. Fate.	Bridgit, Bride, Awen Fortuna	Wheel of Fortune	Nauthiz
Scots Pine	New life, light, illumination. Conception.	Fire Gods Loge (Norse Fire God)	Devil	Kano
Silver Fir (Ailim)	Birth, new beginnings	Artemis Arianrhod Druantia	Star	Fehu
Spruce	Permanence and eternal life	The Great Spirit	World	Othila Gar
Sycamore	Assimilation of new influences	Flora	Temperance	Ehwaz
Willow (Saille)	Moon magic, enchantment, healing, the subconscious	Moon Goddesses Hecate, Circe	Moon	Laguz
Yew (Ioho)	Eternity, death, rebirth, timelessness, change	Banba (Irish death Goddess) Saturn, Ullr	Death	Elhwaz Dagaz Yr

Bibliography

Blum, Ralph. *The Book of Runes*. Michael Joseph Ltd, 1984.

Farrar, Janet & Stewart. *The Witches Way*. Phoenix, 1984.

Graves, Robert. *The White Goddess*. Faber, 1961.

Grieve, Mrs M. *A Modern Herbal*. Penguin 1980.

Herbert, Frank. *Dune*. Victor Gollance 1983.

Hoffman, David, *New Holistic Herbal*. Element, 1983.

Jung, C. *Man and His Symbols*. Picador, 1964.

Kilbracken, John. *Easy Way Guide TREES*. Larousse, 1995.

Man-Ho Kwok (Translator). *Tao Te Ching*. Element Books, 1994.
Naddair, Kaledon. *Keltic Folk and Faerie Tales*. Keltia Publications,1987

Paterson, Jacqueline Memory. *Tree Wisdom*. Harper Collins, 1996.
Pennick, Nigel. *Rune Magic*. Aquarian Press, 1992.

Tolkein, JRR. *Lord of the Rings*. George Allen & Unwin, 1969.

Walters, Martin. *Trees of Britain*. Collins, 1994.

Watson, Lyall. *Gifts of Unknown Things*.

Wilhelm, Richard (Translator). *I Ching*. Routledge & Keegan Paul, 1983.

A selection of other Capall Bann titles. Free catalogue available.

Magical Guardians - Exploring the Spirit & Nature of Trees
by Philip Heselton
This is a book about trees, but a book with a difference, for it acknowledges trees to be wise beings who can teach us much if we approach them in the right way. This book shows how to go about it, revealing the origins of our awakening interest in - and love for - trees. Trees have a spiritual nature, and opening up to this spirit has been a constant feature in human society. Through practical guidance, this book gives hints on how we can make that contact for ourselves. The personalities of the ancient trees - our Magical Guardians - are explored, and the book reveals how we can start to acquire some of their deeper meanings. ISBN 1 86163 057 3   £11.95

Tree: Essence, Spirit and Teacher   by Simon & Sue Lilly
Trees are the creators and maintainers of our reality. In every tradition their spiritual strength has been clearly recognised. Sue and Simon Lilly, developers of *"Green Man Tree Essences"*, share their experiences and describe a wide range of techniques by which we can come into a direct and powerful relationship with the Tree Kingdoms. Emphasis is placed on establishing a personal experience through which the teachings of the Tree Spirits can become apparent. Subjects covered include: The metaphysical reality of trees, Tree essences and how to use them; Meeting the Spirits - methods of communication; Tree Teacher Techniques; Attunements to forty different trees; Coming into the presence of tree energies through initiation, and an exploration of some powerful Tree Teachers. This is the first volume in the *"Tree Seer"* series. ISBN 18163 084 0   £15.95

Tree: Essence of Healing   by Simon & Sue Lilly
The tree is the epitome of balance and stability. Each tree is a window through which we can experience the seamless wholeness of creation, enabling us to re-integrate and repair those aspects of ourselves that have become isolated and damaged. Through the powerful medium of tree essences we have access to the great healing potential of the Tree Kingdoms. This volume explores the qualities of wholeness that trees and tree essences can bring back to the Human Kingdom. Included is a survey of essences and how they work; different ways of healing with trees; an exploration of trees and their healing qualities. ISBN 18163 0816   £14.95

Tree Seer by Simon & Sue Lilly
A workbook designed to direct the reader in the exploration of the Tree Kingdoms. The primary aim is to provide ideas and practical methods to establish a firm basis for direct teaching from the Tree Kingdoms themselves. It encourages flexibility of approach and reliance on experience rather than what others might say or believe. If you want to learn about tree spirits, learn to ask the tree spirits! Includes practical exercises and new material presented in an easy-to-follow layout. ISBN 18163 0824

The Enchanted Forest - The Magical Lore of Trees by Yvonne Aburrow
Fascinating & truly unique - a comprehensive guide to the magical, medicinal & craft uses, mythology, folklore, symbolism & weatherlore of trees. There are chapters on trees in myth & legend, tree spirits, trees in ritual magic, trees & alphabets (runes & Ogham) & weather lore. These chapters are followed by a comprehensive 'herbal index' with in-depth coverage of individual trees from acacia to aspen, wayfaring tree to willow. Profusely illustrated. *"..wonderful insight...easy to read...very informative, a lovely enchanting book"*. Touchstone - the magazine of OBOD, the Order of Bards, Ovates and Druids ISBN 1898307 083   £10.95

Ogham & Coelbren - Mystic Signs and Symbols of the Celtic Druids

by Nigel Pennick
This book explores the "Wattles and the Branches" of the Celtic tree alphabets and tree-lore of the British Isles. It is a wide-ranging explanation of, and commentary on Celtic tree traditions, covering the Oghams of Ireland and the Bardic alphabets of Wales. These symbolic systems encapsulate the ancestral spiritual traditions of the British Isles: their teachings express the Druidic world-view and ways of thought that contemporary education has forgotten. *Ogham & Coelbren* contains the variants of the Irish Ogham tree "alphabet" - its colours, trees, birds and symbols, cryptic codes and hidden inner meanings that encapsulate a creative energy available to-day. The Welsh Bardic system is also detailed, with rare illustrations from scarce texts. A comprehensive appendix details the meanings, correspondences and cosmology that Ogham and Coelbren contain. ISBN 186163   102 2

Sacred Celtic Animals by Marion Davies

Animals affected the everyday lives of the Celts. The Celts saw animals as representations, representatives and messengers of their deities. They took animal names for themselves and their tribes and saw portents and auguries in animals' movements and behaviour. Animals featured extensively in Celtic legends and decorated their weapons, houses and accoutrements. Celtic shamans linked with animals and their warriors and hunters invoked the power of totem animals to help in their endeavours. This book details the myths, legends and correspondences linking the Celts and the animal world. Brilliantly illustrated by Simon Rouse.
ISBN 1898307 75X   £11.95

Dragons of the West by Nigel Pennick

For thousands of years fabulous serpents and dragons have been the stuff of myth and traveller's tales. The dragon has held the attention of people for centuries, and continues to do so. The dragon is more than a beast of tall stories, myth and folk-tale, for it is a symbol of the awesome power of nature which appears in many variant forms, but which we can understand only in symbolic or allegorical form. Thus, it appears in religious symbolism, alchemy, medicine and geomancy as well as in the more lyrical tales of bards and storytellers. Ultimately the dragon is a product of the human mind, for there are dragons of various kinds lurking deep within us all. This book explores Western dragon and dragonslayer traditions, not just legends, but living festivals and rituals surviving today.
ISBN 1 86163 007 7   £10.95

The Mysteries of the Runes by Michael Howard

A full investigation into rune origins, symbolism & use, traced from Neolithic & Bronze Age symbols & their connection with other magical & mystical symbols. Runic divination by Germanic tribes, Saxons and Vikings are also covered. Odin is discussed, as the shaman-god of the runes, with his myths & legends, the Wild Hunt, and the Valkyries. Magical uses of runes are explored with their use in divination. Fascinating information is included on discoveries made in archaeological excavations, rune masters & mistresses, the bog sacrifices of Scandinavia & rune master training. Runic symbolism is detailed together with descriptions of each of the eight runes of Freya's, Haegl's & Tyr's Aetts with divinity, religious symbolism & spiritual meanings based on The Anglo Saxon Rune Poem. How to make your own set of runes, how to cast them for divination with suggested layouts & the use of rune magic. Also covers the gods & goddesses of the Aesir & Vanir, their myths & legends & the seasonal cycle of Northern Tradition festivals. Other topics covered include Hyperborea & the 'Atlantis of the North', duality in Indo-European religion, the Web of Wyrd & the Norns, Saxon/Norse paganism & traditional witchcraft. ISBN 189830 707 5   £9.95

FREE DETAILED CATALOGUE

A detailed illustrated catalogue is available on request, SAE or International Postal Coupon appreciated. **Titles can be ordered direct from Capall Bann, post free in the UK** (cheque or PO with order) or from good bookshops and specialist outlets. Titles currently available include:

Auguries and Omens - The Magical Lore of Birds by Yvonne Aburrow
Caer Sidhe - Celtic Astrology and Astronomy by Michael Bayley
Celtic Lore & Druidic Ritual by Rhiannon Ryall
Earth Dance - A Year of Pagan Rituals by Jan Brodie
Earth Magic by Margaret McArthur
Enchanted Forest - The Magical Lore of Trees by Yvonne Aburrow
Familiars - Animal Powers of Britain by Anna Franklin
Healing Book (The) by Chris Thomas
Handbook For Pagan Healers by Liz Joan
Healing Homes by Jennifer Dent
Herbcraft - Shamanic & Ritual Use of Herbs by S Lavender & A Franklin
In Search of Herne the Hunter by Eric Fitch
Magical Guardians - Exploring the Spirit & Nature of Trees by Philip Heselton
Magical Lore of Cats by Marion Davies
Magical Lore of Herbs by Marion Davies
Patchwork of Magic by Julia Day
Psychic Self Defence - Real Solutions by Jan Brodie
Sacred Animals by Gordon MacLellan
Sacred Grove - The Mysteries of the Forest by Yvonne Aburrow
Sacred Geometry by Nigel Pennick
Sacred Lore of Horses The by Marion Davies
Secret Places of the Goddess by Philip Heselton
Talking to the Earth by Gordon Maclellan
Taming the Wolf - Full Moon Meditations by Steve Hounsome

Capall Bann is owned and run by people actively involved in many of the areas in which we publish. Our list is expanding rapidly so do contact us for details on the latest releases.

Capall Bann Publishing, Freshfields, Chieveley, Berks, RG20 8TF

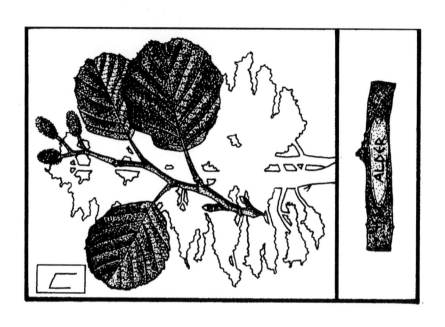

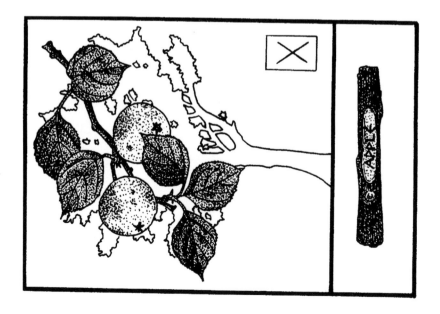

1

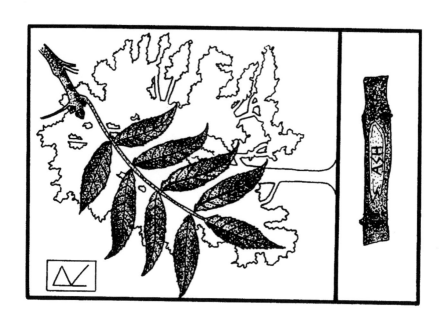

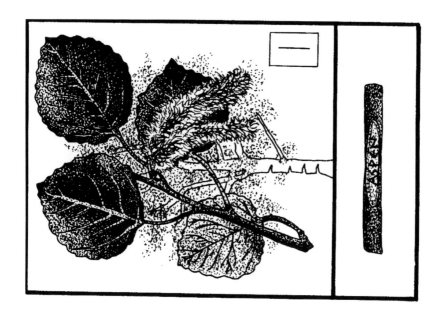

4

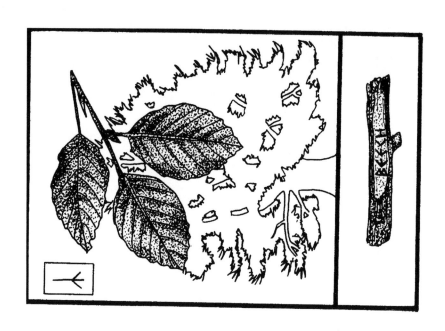

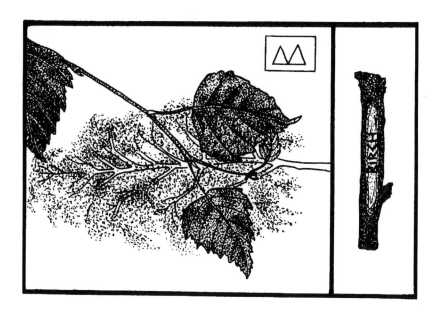

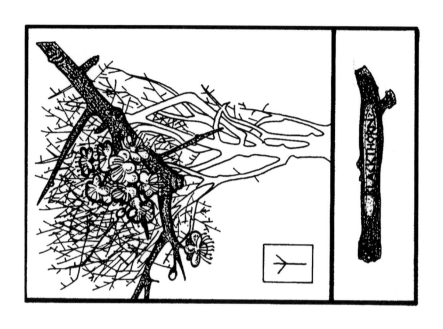

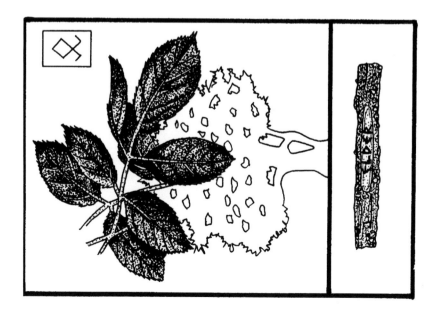

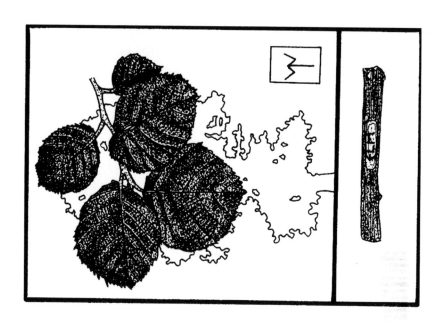

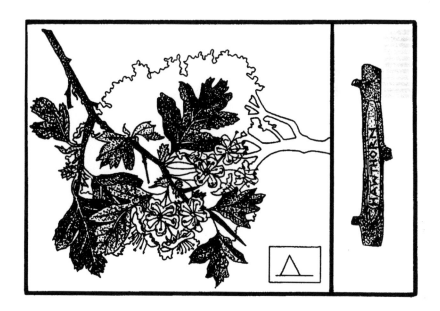

9

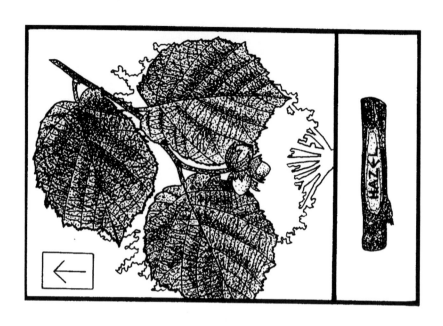

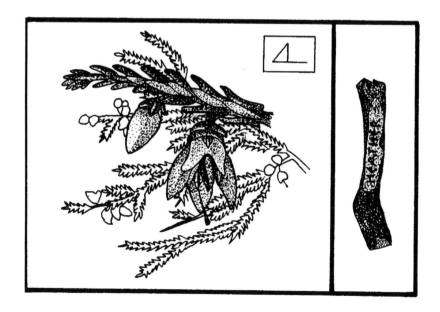

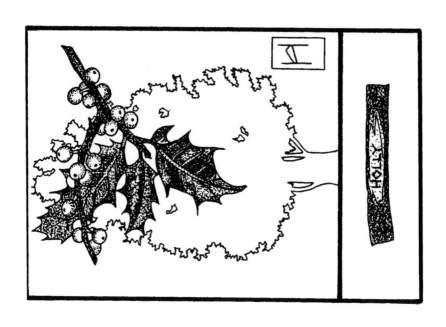

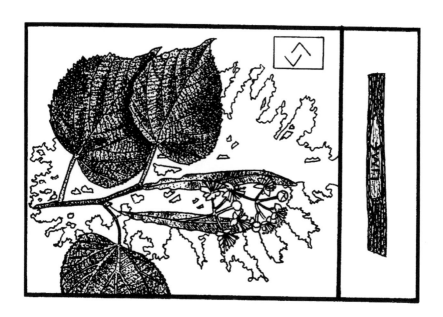

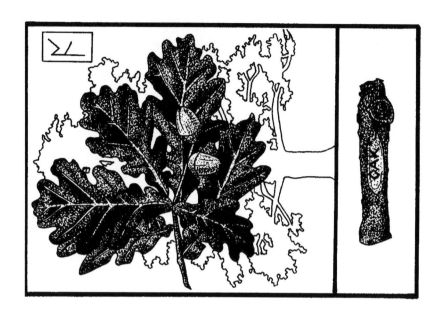

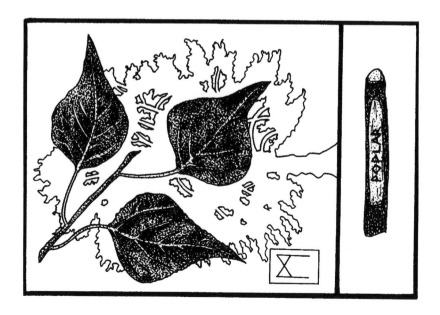

16

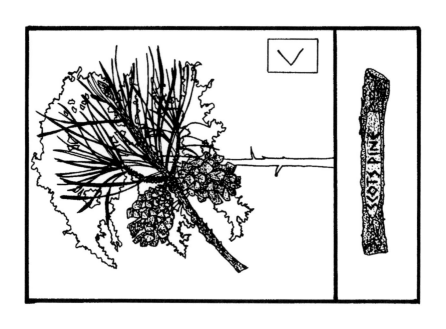

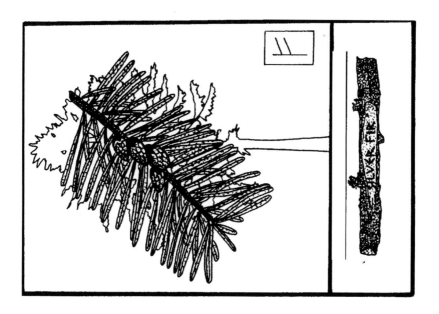

19

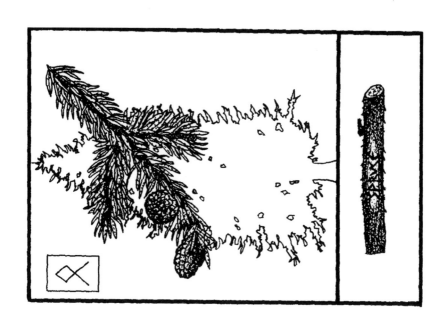

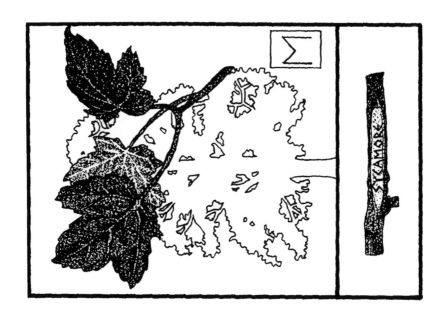

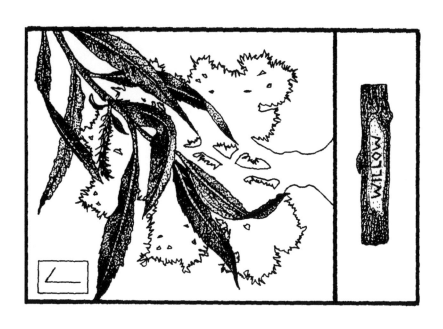

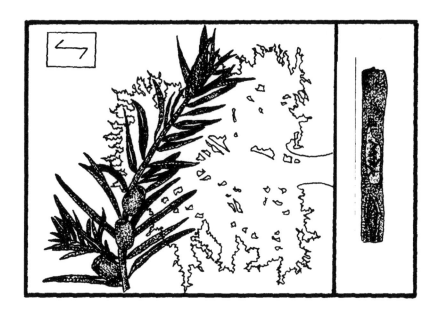